RECEIVING THE
HOLY SPIRIT
AND
HIS GIFTS

by
TERRY VIRGO
and
PHIL ROGERS

RECEIVING THE HOLY SPIRIT AND HIS GIFTS

© Newfrontiers USA 2013

First published in 1990 by Frontier Publishing

Unless otherwise indicated, biblical quotations are from the English Standard Version © 2001 by Crossway, a publishing ministry of Good News Publishers

ISBN 978-0-9814803-5-0

Published by
Newfrontiers USA
PO Box 2626 Saint Louis, MO 63116
www.newfrontiersusa.org

Cover design by Jodi Hertz

Printed in the USA

Thank You To...

I want to thank Phil Rogers for his hard work in the preparation of this material. He is personally responsible for the second half of the book (Chapters 8 – 13) and also worked hard in faithfully reproducing my own teaching material in the first half. The whole book has also been enriched by the additional work of Mary Austin and Chris Wisdom. Thanks also to John Colwell and John Hosier for their useful comments on various theological points. My thanks, too, to Patricia, Phil's secretary, for all her practical help.

Terry Virgo

Other titles by the author:

God's Lavish Grace
La Gracia Abundante de Dios
Enjoying God's Grace
The Spirit-Filled Church
No Well-Worn Paths
Start
Does the Future Have a Church?

Publisher recommended resources on this topic:

Surprised By The Power Of The Spirit, by Jack Deere
Surprised By The Voice Of God, by Jack Deere

Forward

This book has been published with a definite purpose in view. It is a workbook suitable either for housegroups or individuals who want to study the theme of the Holy Spirit in a practical way. The goal is not simply to look up verses and fill up pages of a notebook, but to fill in gaps in our lives and so increase our fruitfulness and our knowledge of God.

Both of Peter's letters were written to "stimulate...wholesome thinking" (2 Peter 3:1). He required his readers to think as well as read! We hope the training manual approach of this book will have the same effect. Stop, think, apply and act are key words.

If you are using the book on your own, I suggest you work through the chapters systematically, Bible and notebook at your side and pen in hand. If you are doing it as a group activity, it is probably best to do all the initial reading and study before the group sessions – this gives more time for discussion on key issues which may be raised.

Unless otherwise stated, all quotations from the Bible are from the English Standard Version.

Terry Virgo

Contents

INTRODUCTION

The "Charismatic Movement" has had a growing impact on the church and the world since the early 1960s. Vast numbers of Christians world-wide have come into an experience of the Holy Spirit formerly unknown to recent generations of Bible-believing churchgoers.

Early shockwaves have been largely forgotten and many are unsure of what it means to be baptized in the Holy Spirit and how one enters into this enduement of power. Some have actually stumbled into a new dimension of the Spirit; some are not sure what has happened to them and others have even wondered if it is a true biblical experience.

"He will baptize you with the Holy Spirit," said John the Baptist as he introduced Jesus to his hearers. Every one of the gospel accounts includes these words and Luke repeats them for good measure in the book of Acts. So there is clear ground on which we can base our faith to receive this promise of the Father.

This book is an attempt to help enquirers know how to receive the Holy Spirit's fullness and an introduction to the gifts of the Holy Spirit, which are available to the church today.

As you work through these pages it is my prayer that you will find your questions answered and your faith quickened to seek the Lord for the promise of the Spirit. I believe that as a result your life can be transformed for the glory of God.

Terry Virgo

YOU SHALL RECEIVE POWER

One day, as I was strolling along Brighton, UK seafront, I saw some people witnessing. I had just been leading the youth group Bible Study and was feeling quite pleased with my performance.

There on the lower promenade were these Pentecostal, grey-haired, frail old ladies holding banners and speaking about Jesus with crackly voices. People were throwing things at them and laughing at them.

I stood there, in my dark glasses, watching what was happening. It was not a pretty sight. "O God, why is it like this?" I thought. Then suddenly I realized that God had called young men like me to do this sort of thing, not frail elderly ladies. "But I'd rather die than do that!" I protested.

There were two guys standing nearby. They were sneering, "Look at those old fools, why don't they keep their religion to themselves?" The Lord prompted me; "At least speak to them about Jesus." But I stood there thinking, "I can't, I just can't do it." I went home broken.

People knew I was a churchgoer, but I was frightened to acknowledge the name of Jesus. I just couldn't speak to people about him. I felt so ashamed, and I was desperate to know how I could overcome my reluctance.

The next morning I phoned a Pentecostal friend and asked him to meet me for lunch near my work place. We often had lunch together and he would always witness to anyone who shared our table. I envied his liberty and admired his boldness. But I almost died every time he spoke about Jesus and wanted him to be quiet. When we parted, I would watch him walking down Oxford Street giving out tracts as he went.

Now I had to see him. I had to know what made him tick. So when we met for lunch I asked him, "How can you witness so freely? What's the secret?" He replied, "I've received the Holy Spirit." So that was the answer to his boldness - the Holy Spirit. I had a knowledge of the Bible and could lead studies, but now I realized that I needed to be filled with the Holy Spirit as well. "I must have what you've got," I told him.

JUST LIKE THOSE DISCIPLES

I felt just like those disciples of Jesus. Initially they thought they were OK. James and John angled for positions at Jesus' right and left hand. Peter

9

said he would never betray or deny Him. But they all denied Him. They all fled. They were all disillusioned and frightened. They all hid behind barred doors. The cross revealed their weakness. But Jesus did not leave them helpless. Later he appeared to them and said:

> **But you will receive power when the Holy Spirit has come upon you, and you will be my witnesses in Jerusalem and in all Judea and Samaria, and to the end of the earth (Acts 1:8).**

This statement has been described as the key to the book of Acts. After the day of Pentecost, this same group of disciples was a dynamic company marching forward with the gospel, traveling all round the Mediterranean, planting powerful churches in one city after another.

What transformed a timid bunch of deserters into a courageous band? How did such fearful believers get such boldness to speak about Christ? They were filled with the Holy Spirit.

Jesus had chosen these men to be his representatives to the world. But before they could ever begin this ministry they had to have God's power. That is why Jesus said:

> **... stay in the city until you are clothed with power from on high (Luke 24:49).**

If we want to fulfill God's plan for our lives, we must have the same experience of the Spirit as the disciples did. God showed me my own need of his power while I was standing on the Brighton seafront. I cried out to him not in aspiration but in desperation! He met me and filled me with his Holy Spirit.

Do you feel your lack of power? God wants to fill you with his Holy Spirit.

GO! BUT WAIT!

After his resurrection Jesus appeared to his disciples and gave them special instructions.

Look up the following verses to see what they were:

Matthew 28:18,19; Mark 16:15; Luke 24:49; Acts 1:4.

Clearly, Jesus was keen to see his disciples spread the gospel. "Here's the commission," he was saying. "Go!" But he did not want them to begin their ministry before they had the power to accomplish it. So Jesus exhorted them to wait in Jerusalem until they had received power from on high.

The Greek word for power is *dunamis* from which we get our words "dynamite", "dynamic" and "dynamo". The root meaning of the word is "to be able". Jesus promised his disciples an "ability" or an "enabling". When the Holy Spirit came upon them, they would receive a dynamic ability that they hadn't had before. They would be given the power of God to enable them to do the work of God.

ANOINTED WITH THE HOLY SPIRIT AND POWER

Jesus told his disciples:

> **As the Father has sent me, even so I am sending you (John 20:21).**

His ministry began with baptism in water, but not only that. Even the Son of God needed power to do his Father's will.

> Read Luke 3:21-2, 4:1,2,14,18 and note the work of the Holy Spirit in Jesus' life.

Jesus did not need to repent of sin so why did he submit to John's baptism of repentance? Here are three reasons.

One, Jesus was anticipating the cross. By going down under the water and rising up from it he identified with the death and resurrection he was going to experience three years later (see Luke 12:50).

Two, by being baptized along with sinners he was identifying himself with sinful man.

Three, he was also saying, "I am dead to the world and to all normal human expectations." The will of God took precedence over everything else. Jesus laid down his life to fulfill it.

When Jesus came up out of the water and was praying, the Holy Spirit descended on him. Peter says that Jesus was "anointed" with the Holy Spirit and power (Acts 10:38). Jesus was not anointed with the ceremonial anointing oil poured over the heads of priests and kings to consecrate them. He was anointed with the heavenly "oil" of the Holy Spirit. Only then was he equipped to begin his ministry.

Jesus refused to entertain Satan's temptations. There would be no short cuts to the purpose of God. Jesus was not interested in Satan's offer of the world and immediate success. He was more concerned about fulfilling God's will for his life.

THE SON OF GOD

Even before he began his ministry Jesus was the perfect Son of God. He had been born of the Holy Spirit - conceived as the Spirit came upon Mary his mother (Matt. 1:20; Luke 1:35). But he did not begin teaching or healing until he had been anointed with power. Until that time Jesus lived in comparative seclusion with his family, working as a carpenter and leading a godly life. But when the Holy Spirit came upon him, he suddenly broke out of anonymity and launched himself into his heavenly Father's business.

Some have said that Jesus' miracles were evidence of his divinity, yet nowhere in the New Testament do we find him acclaimed as God because of signs or miracles. Men in Old Testament days had worked miracles but that did not make them equal with God.

Read John 3:2 and Acts 10:38.

Of what were miracles a sign?

Read John 10:38, 14:10-11; Acts 2:22.

Who is doing the miracles through Jesus?

The Son always works in conjunction with the Father and the Spirit. They exist in eternal interdependence. At the Father's direction, the Son spoke creation into being and the Spirit immediately executed his word of command. So within the Godhead, the Father acts through the Son, by the power of the Holy Spirit.

When Jesus became man he accepted the limitations of our humanity. He depended not on some sort of secret inner force but solely on the power of the Holy Spirit.

When Jesus became man he did not in any way lose his full divinity. He is not God because he has certain attributes or powers. He is God in his very essence. We read that Jesus "made himself nothing" (Phil. 2:7). This literally means, "emptied himself" and is a much debated expression. From it, we understand that Jesus voluntarily laid aside the outward expressions of God-hood. By becoming flesh he emptied himself of his omnipresence (being everywhere), his glory (John 17:5), his omnipotence (having all power) and his omniscience (knowing everything).

So "being made in human likeness. And being found in appearance as a man" (Phil. 2:7-8) Jesus chose to live in obedience to his Father and in full dependence on the power of the Holy Spirit. In this way he became our pioneer, "the firstborn among many brothers" (Rom. 8:29). He is our Savior and our example.

What, according to 1 John 2:6, does God want us to do?

Although Jesus was fully God, he fulfilled his great ministry as a man anointed by the Holy Spirit. This is how the Father sent him; it is also how Jesus sent his disciples.

Read John 14:12.

Who is addressed here?   What is the requirement?
What is the twofold result? Why?

Jesus knew that he would not always be with his disciples in bodily form. But they would not need him if they had his power to complete his work. "I am going away," he said, but added that "the Father ... will give you another counselor to be with you for ever - the Spirit of truth" (John 14:28,16,17). They received the Spirit at Pentecost. He gave them the power to preach and to perform signs and wonders (Acts 2:43).

Consider whether the same power is available to us today.

I WILL POUR OUT MY SPIRIT

Jesus told his disciples to wait until they were clothed with power from on high. They would not have thought this a strange concept because their history was full of people who were given power from God. About half of the eighty or so references to the Spirit in the Old Testament describe this type of experience. Let's look at some of them.

CLOTHED WITH THE SPIRIT

Jesus' disciples knew about David.

Read 1 Samuel 16:13.

What happened when Samuel anointed him?

Some years earlier the Spirit had come upon King Saul and he had prophesied. It was said, "Is Saul also among the prophets?" (1 Sam. 10:11). In those days it was evidently normal for prophets to prophesy when the Spirit came upon them. Even the godless prophet Balaam knew that he could speak only the words that the Spirit gave him.

Read Numbers 24:2-3.

What happened when the Spirit of God came upon him?

The disciples also knew about Samson. When he was a young man the Spirit of the Lord began to stir him (Judg. 13:25), and on a number of occasions gave him extraordinary physical strength.

Read Judges 14:6,19 and 15:14.

What phrase is common to these verses?

The Spirit also came upon other Judges of that period. He came upon Othniel and Jephthah, enabling them to carry out their leadership responsibilities and to defeat Israel's enemies (Judg. 3:10; 11:29).

Perhaps the most well known of the Judges was Gideon. He was a godly young man who, fearing the Midianites, threshed wheat secretly in a wine press.

Read Judges 6:34,35.

What happened when the Spirit came upon this timid man?

Read Judges 6:14-16 and 7:15.

Did he fulfill his commission?

The New International Version says, "The Spirit of the Lord came upon Gideon." However, elsewhere in the Old Testament this same word is usually translated "clothed", "dressed" or "wearing". The phrase literally reads: "the Spirit of the Lord clothed himself with Gideon". He put on Gideon like a suit, dressed himself with Gideon so that he could use him to accomplish God's purposes. The Spirit came upon people in order to work through them.

There are two other places where this word is used in this same way: 1 Chronicles 12: 18 and 2 Chronicles 24:20.

Look up these verses and note how the Spirit used each of the two men.

FILLED WITH THE SPIRIT

When we speak about being "filled with the Spirit" we can slip into the unhelpful notion that God wants to pour a liquid into us. We grin and say,

"Lord, fill me with your Spirit. I leak!" But the Holy Spirit is not a liquid. He is a person. So how can we be full of a person?

The Old Testament idea that the Spirit clothes himself with people is a good illustration here. When I put my clothes on, they are full of me. So when the Holy Spirit comes upon me or clothes himself with me, I am full of the Holy Spirit. When the Spirit of God wears us he can manifest himself in us through what we say and do in response to his prompting. This is how he uses us to fulfill the purposes of God.

The Bible uses a number of different terms to describe this experience. Let's look at the way the various terms are used to describe what happened on the day of Pentecost.

> Following the first example, jot down and consider the different expressions used in the following verses:
>
> Acts 1:5 - baptized with the Holy Spirit
>
> Acts 1:8 -
>
> Acts 2:4 -
>
> Acts 2:17, 33 -
>
> Acts 2:38; 10:47 -
>
> Acts 10:44; 11:15 -

The above terms are all speaking about the same experience of the Holy Spirit. They are therefore used interchangeably throughout this book.

Moses was evidently full of the Spirit of God - although we do not know when he had this experience. Certainly he had some exceptional encounters with God - at the burning bush and later on Mount Sinai when his face radiated God's glory. One very instructive event in his life is recorded in Numbers 11.

> Read verses 10 to 30.

What did God do to Moses and the seventy elders? (v. 17,25)

What did they do? (v. 25)

Moses was extraordinarily privileged. Among the whole nation, only he knew the Spirit of God resting on him, empowering him to lead the people. When the burden became too great for him, God commissioned seventy elders to help him. But before they could share the task they had to be as spiritually equipped as Moses was. We might expect Moses to be jealous that the elders now shared his experience. When Joshua heard Eldad and Medad prophesying in the camp, he was certainly indignant about it.

Consider Moses' response in Numbers 11:29.

Moses' desire then is shared by God now. Here in Numbers we have a most significant anticipation of the New Covenant.

FROM ONE TO ANOTHER

When Moses handed over his responsibilities to Joshua, he laid his hands on him to commission him.

Note what happened when he did this (Deut. 34:9).

With the commission came an impartation of the Spirit that equipped him for his responsibilities. Something similar happened to David when Samuel anointed him with oil (1 Sam. 16:13) and when Elijah left Elisha to continue his ministry.

When the disciples watched Jesus go up into heaven they might well have recalled Elijah's ascension. Elisha knew that God was going to take his master away from him so he kept close to Elijah. There was something he had to have before they were parted.

What did he want? (2 Kings 2:9)

17

Elisha was not being greedy. He was asking for the heir's portion. He was effectively saying, "If I am to take over the ministry that God gave you to do, then I must have the same power that you had." He knew that it was useless to inherit the job without also inheriting the resources necessary to do it. As Elijah was taken up into heaven in the whirlwind, Elisha received his master's anointing and moved on in the power of the Spirit.

When Jesus told his disciples to wait until they had been clothed with power from on high, he was not striking an unfamiliar chord in their hearts. Their scriptures told them that many of God's servants had received the Spirit. Jesus was simply promising them that when he was taken up into heaven, they would inherit his power and be fully equipped to continue the work that he had begun.

THE ANOINTED ONE

Isaiah and other writers of the Old Testament pointed towards the coming of the Messiah or Christ (Hebrew and Greek words for 'Anointed One'). He would be a descendant of King David but would be outstandingly anointed above all others. As "the Lord's anointed", he would receive the Spirit without measure (John 3:34). The Christ would not only be anointed with the Spirit, he would also usher in an age of the Spirit.

Isaiah anticipated a time when the Spirit would be "poured upon us from on high" (Isa. 32:15).

And God himself declared:

> **For I will pour water on the thirsty land, and streams on the dry ground; I will pour my Spirit upon your offspring, and my blessing on your descendants (Isa. 44:3).**

> **And I will not hide my face anymore from them, when I pour out my Spirit upon the house of Israel (Ezek. 39:29).**

Until now, the Old Testament experience of the Spirit was restricted to a very few choice servants of the Lord - people like Moses, Gideon, Samson, the prophets, priests and kings. They were anointed to prophesy, lead or perform some special task.

God's people followed them at a distance because they were the ones with the Spirit. The experience was often only temporary. The Spirit would come upon people for a task and then leave them afterwards. Very few individuals knew anything of the abiding of the Spirit on them.

The day of Pentecost was a landmark between the Old and the New Testaments. When the Spirit came, Joel's prophecy about a widespread outpouring of the Spirit was no longer a future desire - it was a present reality.

What mistakes can you find in the following?

I will pour out my Spirit on some people. Your apostles and elders will prophesy, your house group leaders will dream dreams; your evangelists will see visions. Even on my servants, only women not men, I will pour out my Spirit in those days (Joel 2:28,29).

Moses and the seventy elders, and Elijah and the school of the prophets knew nothing of this widespread outpouring of the Spirit. Their experience was a shadow of something much greater – a time when God would pour out his Spirit on every one of his people and accomplish his purposes through them all.

(3)

HE WILL BAPTIZE YOU WITH THE HOLY SPIRIT

WHY JESUS CAME

God sent John the Baptist to prepare the way for the Anointed One. John made two statements about why Jesus came. The first is recorded only in John's Gospel. According to John the Baptist, Jesus came to:

take away the sin of the world (John 1:29).

The second statement is found in all four of the Gospels and in Acts 1. He said that Jesus came to:

baptize ... with the Holy Spirit and with fire (Matt. 3:11).

Most evangelical Christians tend to reverse the emphasis. They focus almost exclusively on Jesus as Savior, not as the one who ushers in a new age – the "ministry of the Spirit" (2 Cor. 3:8).

In view of these things, it is surprising that during his three years of ministry, Jesus said so very little about the Holy Spirit. Certainly, the Spirit is mentioned significantly in the early chapters of Matthew and Luke, but after Jesus' anointing, all we have is a comment here and there. One clue to the reason for this lies in a statement made by Jesus, which is recorded in Luke 12:49,50:

I came to cast fire on the earth, and would that it were already kindled! I have a baptism to be baptized with, and how great my distress until it is accomplished!

Jesus was effectively saying, "Yes, I have come to baptize with fire. I'm longing to pour out my Spirit. But before I can do that I must go through a baptism of my own - on the cross. I must be the sacrificial lamb of God. I must first atone for sin because only then can I baptize with the Holy Spirit."

Redemption was only part of God's purpose for us. Paul says that:

[God redeemed us] so that in Christ Jesus the blessing of Abraham might come to the Gentiles, so

20

that we might receive the promised Spirit through faith (Gal. 3:14).

The cross was not an end in itself, but the means to a greater end. God wants to justify people, give them Christ's righteousness, fill them with his Spirit and make them a blessing to the nations.

Just as Moses saved his people from their bondage in Egypt, so Jesus delivers us from our bondage to sin. Just as Joshua brought the people into the Promised Land, so Jesus (whose name is a form of Joshua) brings us the promised Holy Spirit. Just as the Israelites were given a land flowing with milk and honey, so we can be filled with the fullness of God.

I AM GOING AWAY

The Gospels suggest that Jesus said comparatively little about the Spirit until the night before his crucifixion. Then, knowing that he would soon be taken from his disciples, he gathered them together for what we call the Upper Room discourse (John 13-17) and began to teach them about the Spirit.

Read John 14:16,17 and consider:

Who cannot receive the Spirit?

Where God wants the Spirit to be.

Read John 14:26 and 15:26.

Note what the Spirit will do.

Read John 16:7 and imagine what happens if Jesus does not go away.

"It is for your good that I am going away," said Jesus. Such a statement must have stunned the disciples who had been his constant companions for three years. They had seen the crowds flock to hear him and had witnessed the most amazing sights: lepers cleansed, the sick healed and people delivered from demons and even raised from the dead. Every question he answered. Every need he met. Yet now he was saying, "It is for your good that I am going away." Surely, it would be far better if he stayed! But Jesus wanted to raise their faith. "It is better for the Holy Spirit to be with you," he was saying. Later they realized why.

When Jesus was on earth he could only be in one place at one time. When he was in Jerusalem he could not be in Capernaum, and when he was in Capernaum he could not be in Bethany.

The Jews thought that by killing Jesus they would rid the world of his influence. But then the Holy Spirit fell on his disciples and Jesus, by the Spirit, was present with them wherever they went. So at the same time, Peter could be in Joppa, Philip in Samaria and Paul in Antioch and Jesus could be in all three places at once! The same power that was with Jesus rested on his followers, enabling them to teach and perform amazing miracles.

The Holy Spirit is omnipresent, which means, "all present" or "everywhere at the same time". This does not mean that he is thinly spread everywhere. When Peter and John went up to the temple, Jesus was with them - and a cripple was healed. When Philip went to Samaria Jesus went there too and many believed and were healed.

That was why Jesus said that it was better for him to go away than to stay. The things that he had done they would do – and even greater things than these. Why? Because he was going to the Father.

> Read Acts 2:33 and consider the two things that happened
> when Jesus was exalted to the right hand of God.

WAIT IN JERUSALEM

The disciples' success was wrapped up in Jesus' return to the Father. It was imperative that they wait in Jerusalem until Jesus sent them the Holy Spirit.

God does not give us the Spirit so that we can enjoy a few more up-tempo songs. He gives us the power that Jesus had to live as he lived, to speak as he spoke and to do what he did. He is looking for a church that will reach the nations with the gospel. When that has been accomplished, the end will come and Jesus will return in triumph for a church that has done the job he commissioned us to do.

When we understand the immensity of the task, we become acutely aware of our lack of power. We think, "If Elisha needed power to follow the ministry of Elijah, how much more do I need Jesus' power to continue the ministry of Jesus? If I'm going to accomplish great things for him, I must have the Spirit that he had."

"So what am I meant to do?" we ask. "I'm a Christian, did I automatically receive the Spirit when I believed? Should I imitate the early disciples and wait for the power? Do I need the laying on of hands? What must I do to receive the Spirit? Where do I go from here?"

After I became aware how much I needed the power of the Spirit, I began to read book after book about the subject. But people's opinions tended to confuse me.

CONFUSING THEORIES

Depending on whom you ask, you will encounter a variety of responses to this dilemma. Let's look at four theories.

GRADUAL FILLING

Some people say, "You automatically receive everything at conversion. You gradually become more mature as you increasingly yield yourself to the Spirit within you. So being filled with the Spirit is a process."

HIGHER LIFE

Others suggest, "Initially you accept Jesus as your Savior but later you surrender yourself to him as Lord. Then his Spirit fills you more and gives you the ability to live a higher life." A popular illustration of this likens us to a glass that is full of "self". When you empty it out God can fill it with his Spirit. This full surrender and emptying of yourself is a kind of sanctification crisis. When you totally give yourself to God in this way his Spirit can fill you and you enter into the higher life.

RELEASE

Some maintain that we receive everything at conversion or at baptism or confirmation, but there comes a time when we appropriate the gift that we have already received. This is referred to as "the release of the Spirit". The Spirit may be locked up within us for many years, but may

23

later be released through a crisis experience.

At that time we step out in faith and exercise the gift of the Spirit within us by reaching out to the sick or speaking in tongues.

TARRYING

There are some who declare, "The disciples had to wait In Jerusalem for the Spirit to be poured out upon them. That's what you have to do too - possibly for years - and when you speak in tongues you will know you have been baptized in the Spirit." In the past, people would go to tarrying meetings to pray and seek God for this to happen to them. They would repent and pray and fast and try to be holy in order to make themselves fit to receive the Spirit. Some waited for years and never spoke in tongues.

Faced with such diverse theories, what are we to believe? How can we be filled with the Spirit? In our next chapter we shall see what happened to the earliest Christians.

THE SPIRIT IN ACTS

God wants us to build his church on the pattern of the one in the New Testament. Much modern church life is unrecognizable when compared with the early church because of so-called "historical development" – which is actually historical deviation.

The New Testament tells us how we should function and what we should experience. Some say that we cannot establish doctrine from narrative passages in the Bible, arguing that we must focus on the solid teaching in the epistles and on Jesus' words in the gospels. But this belief undermines the truth of 2 Timothy 3:16 which declares that:

All Scripture is breathed out by God and profitable for teaching, for reproof, for correction, and for training in righteousness.

God did not have the inspired book of Acts preserved purely for the sake of historical interest. If the Old Testament narratives were written to instruct us (1 Cor. 10:11), surely the New Testament account of our church origins is of equal or even greater value. We ignore to our detriment the ministry of our predecessors, the ones who paved the way and show us how to walk in the purposes of God.

The book of Acts is of vital importance to today's church and we would benefit from reading it again and again. It inspires and motivates us with a realistic picture of our calling and destiny. In it we discover how the early Christians first received the Spirit and how their experience provides a pattern for us today.

ACTS 2

Since this outstanding passage is so familiar, we will not spend a great deal of time on it.

Read through the chapter now to familiarize yourself with its contents.

Acts 2 documents the first outpouring of the Spirit. About a hundred and twenty people were gathered in one place when they were suddenly clothed with power from on high. The Spirit fell upon them and they all began to worship God and speak with tongues. Following this experience, they became a dynamic, forceful company who turned the world upside down.

ACTS 8

The second account of the outpouring of the Spirit occurs in Samaria.

Read Acts 8: 1 2-17 and consider:

What Philip was preaching.

Whether people actually became Christians.

Why Peter and John were sent to them.

Why this was necessary.

What they did and what the result was.

There is no mention here that the new converts spoke in tongues or prophesied. But Simon the Sorcerer saw something happen to them that so impressed him that he offered the apostles money saying, "Give me also this ability so that everyone on whom I lay my hands may receive the Holy Spirit" (v. 19). There must have been some sort of manifestation to impress him so much.

ACTS 9

In this chapter we read of the apostle Paul's conversion. He was on the road to Damascus when the Lord came to him in a blinding light. Three days later, Ananias visited him.

Read verse 17.

What were the first two words that Ananias said to Paul (Saul)? What does this say about Paul's spiritual state? Why did Ananias visit Paul?

Who was Ananias? Was he some great apostle like Peter? No. He was just an ordinary believer who obeyed Jesus. We have never heard of him before and we never hear of him again. But he was chosen to minister to the man who would one day become the most significant of all the apostles.

ACTS 10

The next outpouring of the Holy Spirit took place in the house of a man called Cornelius. Peter would never have set foot in this Gentile home unless God had told him to do so. God overcame Peter's scruples by giving him a vision of unclean food – unclean to the Jewish mind that is – and commanding him to eat. While he was pondering this vision, God told Peter that he had sent three men to see him. Peter welcomed them and the next day went with them to Cornelius" home. When he arrived he spoke to those assembled about Jesus. But while Peter was still speaking, something extraordinary and unexpected happened. The Holy Spirit fell on them.

Why were the circumcised (Jewish) believers so astonished? (Acts 10:45)

How did they know what had happened? (v. 46)

On what basis did Peter order them to be baptized? (v. 47)

Here we see a different sequence of events. Peter was preaching the gospel message to the unbelievers who had gathered. While was doing this, faith was rising in their hearts and they were agreeing that Jesus was the Christ. Then the Spirit fell on them. There was no delay, no three day gap, no tarrying! They were born again and filled with the Holy Spirit

27

all in a moment. Peter did not even get the chance to finish speaking, let alone lay hands on them! Yet the same supernatural things were happening now as they had in the upper room on the day of Pentecost.

When Peter returned to Jerusalem, he faced criticism from the Jewish believers who wanted to know why he was associating with the Gentiles. Peter effectively said, "But I never touched them! I never laid a hand on them! While I was speaking, the Holy Spirit fell on them just as he had fallen on us. It was the Lord, not me! If you have questions, you had better take them up at a higher level!"

I believe that this is the reason why the account of Cornelius' conversion is so different from the others. God had to prove to the Jewish believers that he wanted to include the Gentiles in his purposes. So God had to break in sovereignly and unexpectedly in order to change their thinking.

In John 3:8 the Spirit is likened to wind.

Where does this wind blow? What do you hear? What can't you tell?

Cornelius' experience warns us not to be too dogmatic about the way the Spirit moves. The Spirit is likened to wind, fire and water - all unpredictable elements. So when we are developing a doctrine of the Holy Spirit and his ways, we can really only say, "It's usually like this." As soon as we try to define him too much, he will do something unexpected.

Not only must we avoid being too dogmatic about the Spirit, we must also beware of the opposite extreme and fall into a sort of mysticism, which says, "Who can know anything about the Spirit? We'll just have to see what happens." The Bible gives us objective truth about the Spirit and how he operates. It describes his activities and gives us a basis for expectation. But we must leave room for him to break in sovereignly on us – as he did in the life of Cornelius.

ACTS 19

The final account of the outpouring of the Spirit is found in Acts 19 (although we have not looked at Acts 4 where the Spirit filled again those who had earlier received him at Pentecost).

Arriving at Ephesus, Paul found a group of disciples and began talking to them.

> Read Acts 19:1-7.
>
> Paul must have sensed that there was something lacking in these men, which is why he quizzed them.
>
> What question did he ask them? (v. 2)
>
> What was their reply? (v. 2)
>
> What was Paul's next question? (v. 3)

If these men had received Christian baptism they would have heard about the Holy Spirit. It was all part of the same package Peter had outlined on the day of Pentecost:

> **Repent and be baptized every one of you in the name of Jesus Christ for the forgiveness of your sins, and you will receive the gift of the Holy Spirit (Acts 2:38).**
>
> **John baptized with the baptism of repentance, telling the people to believe in the one who was to come after him, that is, Jesus (Acts 19:4).**

People from all over Palestine went out to hear John the Baptist. These men in Ephesus had evidently heard his message; either directly from the prophet himself or from someone like Apollos (see Acts 18:24,25). They would have known about the Coming One who would take away sins and baptize in the Spirit – because that was John's message. Apollos taught accurately about Jesus, though he knew only the baptism of John. Priscilla and Aquila had to take him aside and explain the way of God more adequately (Acts 18:26).

Paul also had to explain the way of God to these men too. When he told them about Jesus they readily believed, and were baptized into Jesus' name (v. 5). Whatever had been deficient in their previous experience

29

was now made up. But notice that Paul did not leave it there.

What did he do next? What happened?

There was a gap between conversion and the outpouring of the Spirit at Pentecost, in Samaria and in the experience of Paul. Here these men were converted and filled with the Spirit on the same day, although their experience differed from that of Cornelius. In whatever way God chose to work, there are three distinct elements present: 1) hearing the gospel, 2) believing in the Lord Jesus and 3) receiving the Holy Spirit.

Paul underlined this progression in his letter to the Ephesians (which would have included this original group of a dozen men). He wrote:

> **In Him, you also, after listening to the message of truth, the gospel of your salvation – having also believed, you were sealed in him with the Holy Spirit of promise (Eph. 1:13 NASB).**

First they had heard the message of truth, the good news of their salvation, secondly they had believed and then they had been sealed with the promised Holy Spirit. The process is this:

Hearing – believing – receiving the Spirit.

As we have seen, these elements may all happen together or there may be minutes, hours or days between them. The question is, have you experienced them all? Let me repeat Paul's question of Acts 19:2.

Did you receive the Holy Spirit when you believed?

RECEIVING THE SPIRIT

So how do you receive the Spirit? We have looked briefly at the theories, but how do they square with the experiences that people had in the book of Acts? Let's see.

GRADUAL FILLING

Do we automatically receive everything at conversion? Certainly, Cornelius' story indicates that an individual can be saved and filled with the Spirit at the same time. But for Paul and those in Samaria and Ephesus, the case was very different. They heard the Gospel and believed it, but they received the Spirit later through the laying on of hands. Clearly the teaching that we automatically receive the Spirit at conversion is not borne out by these examples in the book of Acts.

Coupled with this notion that we receive everything at conversion is the idea that being filled with the Spirit is something that happens gradually. If you ask someone who holds this view, "Have you been filled with the Spirit?" he will usually reply, "As I walk with God and grow in grace I'm steadily being more and more filled with the Spirit." This may sound spiritual but it is not biblical.

When Paul asked the Ephesian disciples if they had received the Spirit, they didn't say. "We're steadily moving into the fullness." They were quite clear that they had not had this experience. But if Paul had asked the same question after he had laid his hands on them, they would have responded with a very definite, "Yes!"

In the New Testament, the people were not vaguely aware of the Spirit. Either they had received him or they had not. When the Spirit came upon them they knew all about it and so did everyone else present. Simon the Sorcerer saw something happen and wanted to buy the ability to give the Spirit. Certainly we need to grow in grace, but this has nothing to do with receiving the Holy Spirit.

HIGHER LIFE

Is there a later step of sanctification? Do we receive Jesus as our

Savior at conversion and then, as we grow in our understanding of God and our weakness, bow the knee and accept him as Lord? Is the filling of the Spirit linked with a new kind of surrender?

Certainly, Christians do give themselves to God more fully; they deal with their sin; they know a greater reality of God and may even have an experience of being filled with the Spirit. But the idea that there is a "higher life" is neither taught nor demonstrated in the entire New Testament. Nowhere do we find the apostles saying, "It's great that you've made Jesus your Savior and have been baptized. Later, as you grow in your faith, you will need to make Jesus your Lord, then you will receive the fullness of the Spirit."

What do we confess at conversion? (Rom. 10:9)

If you cannot confess this, then it could be questioned whether you are a Christian at all.

Peter and Paul did not tell new converts, "Now, you must wait until you have a more mature grasp of your salvation before you ask for the Spirit." Not a bit of it! Immediately the new believers were baptized, the apostles laid hands on them and expected them to receive the Spirit - which they did.

Some people have protested, "Isn't this rather dangerous? Shouldn't we hesitate to furnish young Christians with such power and gifts? That's rather like giving a loaded gun to a small child. The wisest course of action must be to wait until people are more mature and can handle such things."

Paul did not seem to think like that. The church at Corinth was in a mess, but Paul said:

> **I give thanks to my God always for you... that in every way you were enriched in him in all speech and all knowledge ... so that you are not lacking in any spiritual gift (1 Cor. 1:4-7).**

Paul's way of handling their immaturity was not to say, "Wait until you're more experienced and can cope with these spiritual things." On the contrary, he effectively told them, "Here's the dynamite. This is how you use it properly. Get on with it and God will sanctify you as you go."

God wants us to be zealous about maturity, but he does not want us to think that by trying to be holy we can somehow earn his power and a gift or two. This is not a biblical idea. God loves to lavish his gifts upon all Christians - the young, the middle-aged, the old and even the irresponsible! Indeed, we are currently seeing all sorts of amazing signs and wonders in very young churches –particularly in the so-called "Third World".

RELEASE

Do we receive the gift of the Spirit at our "Christian initiation" (conversion, baptism or confirmation) and then seek to "release" the Spirit from within us? According to the New Testament - No!

When Peter and John went to Samaria they did not tell the newly baptized believers, "You've been baptized, so you've got the Spirit, now just release him. Speak out in tongues." We know that the new converts were believers but we also know that "The Holy Spirit had not yet come upon any of them" (Acts 8:16). Only when Peter and John laid hands on them did they receive the Spirit.

Consider the following false statement:

When Paul placed his hands on them, the Holy Spirit welled up from within them, and they spoke in tongues and prophesied.

You will find the correct version in Acts 19:6.

Do you get the point?

TARRYING

Must we wait for the Spirit? When I was first seeking the Spirit some friends told me that I should "tarry" until something happened. I met people who had been "tarrying" for ages. One of them had been waiting ten years but had received nothing.

Those of us who have recently been involved in the charismatic movement may find these things hard to believe. But a few years ago, tarrying meetings were important among Pentecostals if you earnestly wanted to receive the Spirit. The people who attended them kept pleading with God to fill them. They were saying to themselves, "When I speak in tongues I'll believe I've got it, but until I speak in tongues, I won't believe." Although they did not realize it, they were actually putting the cart before the horse. They were looking for a sign before they believed, when God wanted them to believe because he had promised.

Why did they teach the need to tarry? Because Jesus told the disciples to stay in the city until they had been clothed with power from on high (Luke 24:49). At Pentecost we see the result of this waiting.

> **And they were all filled with the Holy Spirit and began to speak in other tongues as the Spirit gave utterance (Acts 2:4).**

The filling of the Spirit was evidenced in the gift of tongues. After the day of Pentecost, no one was ever again told to wait. When Ananias was sent to Paul he did not say, "Now Paul, you're going to be an apostle. Since all the other apostles had to wait for the Spirit, you'd better find a nice quiet upper room somewhere and do the same. The power will come eventually." No! He went up to Paul, laid his hands on him and the Spirit immediately came upon him. Similarly, after Paul had baptized the men in Ephesus, he laid his hands on them and they were instantly filled with the Holy Spirit.

So why did Jesus tell the disciples to wait for the Spirit? The Bible teaches us that they were not waiting until they were ready; they were waiting until Jesus was ready.

The outpouring of the Spirit was dependent not upon the performance of the disciples but on the position of their Savior. Until Jesus had been exalted to the right hand of God, he could not pour out the Spirit. That is why they had to wait.

> Read Acts 2:38,39 and identify the four groups of people who may receive the promise of the Holy Spirit.
>
> Are you included?

Having established that the outpouring of the Holy Spirit flows from the ascended and glorified Christ, let's see how we can receive the gift for ourselves.

IF ANYONE IS THIRSTY

The Feast of Tabernacles lasted a whole week. Every day, water from the Pool of Siloam was ceremonially poured out in the center of Jerusalem to symbolize God's provision. The last day of the feast was the greatest day - the choicest time for Jesus to stand and declare himself to be the source of living water and the one who would pour out the Holy Spirit. Jesus said:

> **If anyone thirsts, let him come to me and drink. Whoever believes in me, as the Scripture has said, 'Out of his heart will flow rivers of living water' (John 7:37-39).**

If you had been there at the feast, you might have gone up to Jesus and said, "Yes, Lord. I'm thirsty for your Spirit. I want him to flow through me. Please give him to me." Had you done that, you would have been disappointed. Jesus would have responded, "I'm sorry. I can't give you the Spirit now."

Hearing this you might have protested, "Why not now? Didn't you promise...? Am I disqualified for some reason? Why can't I receive the Spirit now?" In reply, Jesus would have said, "It's nothing to do with you. I'd love to give you the Spirit now but I can't. You must wait."

According to John 7:39 why couldn't Jesus have given you the Spirit?

On the high day of another feast, the Feast of Pentecost, Jesus poured out the Holy Spirit upon his church. Did he delay because they needed time to prepare themselves to receive the Spirit? No. They had to wait until Jesus was ready. Only when he was exalted in heaven could he fulfill his promise and give the Spirit to his church.

Let faith rise in your heart. The Spirit is given because Jesus has been glorified. No one need ever wait for the outpouring of the Spirit again.

JESUS IS WORTHY

When we start seeking the outpouring of the Spirit, the devil will do all he can to discourage us. He does not want to see Christians full of the Holy Spirit and will try to make us look in at ourselves and despair at what we see. "It's OK for others," we conclude. "I'm just not good enough."

The devil is quick to agree. "I saw what you did the other day," he says. "Call yourself a Christian? You're not worthy to receive the Spirit." We then embark on a strict self-preparation program which includes things like Bible study, prayer, fasting, confession, self-surrender and general waiting for it to happen.

I do not want to discourage anyone from praying or fasting or hungering after God. But the believers in the New Testament were never told, "You must make yourself worthy to receive the Spirit." What we are is not the issue. Our focus must be on the one who is worthy. Jesus is the Lamb of God who has taken away our sin. He is now glorified and has received from the Father the promised Holy Spirit. He wants us all to be filled with the Spirit and is ready to give the gift to anyone who wants it.

LIVING PROOF THAT JESUS IS ALIVE

Jesus told his disciples:

> **you will receive power when the Holy Spirit has come upon you, and you will be my witnesses (Acts 1:8).**

This does not mean that when we are baptized in the Spirit we will suddenly become fantastic orators! The Scripture speaks of our being witnesses, not doing witnessing. If you are a witness, you have see something, you can testify to what you know and give evidence that it is true.

Every Spirit-filled person is proof that Jesus is not a corpse rotting in a tomb in the Middle East. Dead men cannot give the Holy Spirit. Only someone who has ascended to the right hand of the Father on high can do that. So when we are full of the Holy Spirit we automatically become witnesses to Jesus' resurrection and ascension. We are living proof to the world that Jesus is alive. Peter said:

> **He [Jesus] has poured out this that you yourselves are seeing and hearing (Acts 2:33).**

The evidence of Jesus' resurrection was right before the eyes of the crowd.

THE SPIRIT IS ACCESSIBLE

Jesus once said, "If anyone is thirsty, let him come to me and drink." But he did not mean, "Come now." He meant, "Not yet. Not until I'm glorified." Since Jesus has been glorified the "not yet" clause no longer applies. There is a waterfall of God's grace and power available for us right now.

I remember speaking to a couple about this many years ago. I was taking them through various passages of Scripture and we were about three quarters of the way through the evening. I was about to bring it all to a conclusion when the husband asked his wife to make some coffee. She went into the kitchen, but before she had finished making the coffee she ran back in declaring, "It's wonderful! It's wonderful!"

We asked her what had happened and she replied, "The Holy Spirit has come upon me." I hadn't even finished my explanation! I hadn't laid hands on her. But she had understood and believed and reached out to Jesus. You can receive the Spirit before you finish reading these words. The Spirit is available – to you.

IF ANYONE IS THIRSTY

Are you thirsty? I hope so. You probably would not be reading this book If you were not thirsty for God. Jesus did not say, "If anyone is holy" or "If anyone is special" or "If anyone is a super-saint". He was looking for thirsty people.

God made me thirsty by showing me the desperate need in the world and my inability to communicate Jesus with those who did not know Him. After that painful experience on the Brighton seafront I became extremely thirsty. Have you become thirsty?

LET HIM COME TO ME

The weekend after my lunch appointment with my Pentecostal friend, I joined him at his church and sat in a circle with others who were seeking the baptism of the Spirit. A man was laying hands on each person and praying for the power of God to come on them. Seeing the joy on their faces, I thought, "This looks good. This is why I came. I'm going to receive the Spirit through this man."

Then he laid hands on me, prayed and went on to the next one. Everyone around me was worshiping and encouraging me to do the same. But I was thinking, "Hey, wait a minute! What's all this? Come back! Nothing has happened." People around me were saying, "Praise the Lord." But I was thinking, "Why praise the Lord? Nothing has happened! Then they exhorted me, "Say 'Hallelujah!'" By this time I was thinking, "This is desperate! I've come all this way to meet with God. These people are trying to get me excited and I'm dead on the inside."

Why was this happening to me? Perhaps because at that moment my faith focused on a man when I should have been going to Jesus. The man had no power of his own. He could not fill me with the Spirit. Only Jesus could do that. By all means ask someone for the laying on of hands for the Spirit but remember to look beyond the servant to the Master. You must make sure you come to Jesus.

AND DRINK

Jesus did not say "and beg". He did not tell us to prostrate ourselves before him and plead, "Oh God! Oh Jesus! Please give me your Holy Spirit. Please do it for me. Oh Lord! Please! Please!" He said, "Come to, me and drink." "Take it," he is saying. "Just come and receive."

God is a loving Father who wants to give us his Spirit (Luke 11:11-13). He wants us to ask with the expectation of receiving. We do not have to plead and beg but neither do we sit back passively and just wait. We drink.

Suppose it is a hot sunny day. My young children are playing in the garden when they hear an ice cream van playing its tune in the neighborhood. They race in and say, "Dad, can we have an ice cream?" Knowing that I can be stingy, they are probably thinking as they ask me, "Not a chance!" And of course I say, "Not on your life!"

Suppose the following day is equally hot. I am looking out of the window at the kids as they play in the sweltering heat and I am thinking, "Poor things, they'd love something nice and cool." So I go in the car, drive to the shops, buy some ice cream and drive home again. Then I open the back door and call out, "Hey! Come and get your ice cream!" Before I know it my youngsters are all round me asking for their refreshments. I went to a great deal of trouble to make them available, and my children come to me with confidence that I will give them an ice cream because it was my idea, not theirs.

The baptism of the Spirit is not our idea, but God's. Jesus went to an enormous amount of trouble to make it available to you. He removed your sin and ascended into heaven where he received the promised Holy

Spirit from his Father. Now he says to you, "Are you thirsty? Come to me and drink."

God knows your heart. He understands your doubts. You question: "Does God really want to give this to me?" And he replies:

Ask, and it will be given to you (Luke 11:9).

He also understands your fears - You wonder, "What will happen to me if I yield to this? Will I fall on the floor? Will I shake about uncontrollably?" and you conclude: "I'm not sure if I really want the Hoooly Ghooost!" But God reminds you that he is more loving and faithful to you than your earthly father. He will not give you something that is dangerous or spooky - any more than a good father would.

Read Luke 11:12,13.

Consider the way that a good father responds to his children when they ask him for things.

If you ask your heavenly Father for the Holy Spirit, what will he give you?

Are you thirsty?

Jesus offers you a drink.

Take it.

THE STEP OF FAITH

Jesus calls thirsty people to come to him and drink. Then he goes on to say, "Whoever believes in me..." Clearly, the exercise of faith is vitally important when we come to receive the Holy Spirit.

Answer the question posed in Galatians 3:5.

The New American Standard version translates the last few words of this verse: "by hearing with faith". There is a faith element to receiving the Spirit, so we have to shake off passivity.

When they were praying for me to receive the Spirit and exhorting me to praise the Lord, I was desperate for something to happen to me. The trouble was that I was passive. "I'm not going to make up some silly language," I told myself. Then they took me back to the promises in God's Word and showed me how faithful he is to give to all who ask. As I listened I began to believe God for his Spirit. "Surely..." I thought, "...the Lord has brought me this far. I can't believe that he wants me to go home empty." So instead of sitting there passively waiting for something to happen, I reached out to the Lord and began to drink and to believe.

Faith without action is dead (James 2:17). It is not real faith at all. Many miracles in the Bible happened when people actively responded to the Word.

If we had been standing with the Israelites on the edge of the River Jordan we might have been tempted to fast and pray all night for God to part the waters.

Read Joshua 3:8-16 and consider:

What God told the priests to do.

What God promised would happen.

Whether the priests heard with faith.

Whether God fulfilled his promise.

When Jesus told the ten lepers to "Go, show yourselves to the priests" (Luke 17:14), they probably looked at their hands and feet and said, "What's the point of doing that? Nothing's happened!"

When were they cleansed?

"Stretch out your hand," said Jesus to a man whose hand was withered, (Matt. 12:13). I can imagine the poor man saying to himself, "That's my problem. I can't stretch it out." But what did he do? He did what he knew he could not do. He heard Jesus, reached out in faith and found that he could do what he could not!

Jesus said to a paralytic, "Get up, take your mat and go home" (Mark 2:11). He said to a man born blind, "Go ... wash in the Pool of Siloam" (John 9:7). They heard him and said to themselves "Jesus says I can do it and I believe him!" They heard with faith. Jesus wants you to hear with faith as you come to him for the outpouring of the Holy Spirit.

Jesus' promise of the Spirit was based on what the Scripture had said. God had declared that he would pour out the Spirit on all flesh. He is the source of living water. Jeremiah took up this theme, but what he said to the people was not encouraging:

Be appalled, O heavens, at this; be shocked, be utterly desolate... my people have committed two evils. (Jeremiah 2:2-13a)

Read Jeremiah 2:12,13.

What were those sins?

Sadly, some Christians are doing the same thing today. They are neglecting the power of the Spirit and trying to serve God out of their own resources. They are so busy striving to please God by works of evangelical law that they fail to realize that what they are digging does not hold water. They have forsaken the spring of living water. They are devoid of the power of God.

41

Many of them have never received the Spirit's power simply because they have never been told about it. Like the twelve men at Ephesus they have not heard that the Holy Spirit is available. They have been led to believe that they must automatically have received the fullness of the Spirit at conversion. Assuming that their experience is normal, they restrict all supernatural activities to the Bible.

If preachers do not preach about the availability of the Spirit's power, Christians will not hear it. If they do not hear it, they cannot believe and receive it. On the other hand, when Christians are taught these truths from the Scriptures and hear with faith, they will receive the Holy Spirit.

A young married couple was in leadership in a church where the teaching emphasis was: "You received everything at conversion". The use of tongues was forbidden and no other viewpoint tolerated. Then they attended a conference where a large number of the delegates were Spirit-filled. They enjoyed the lively worship but could not enter into it themselves. When they began asking questions about receiving the Spirit, we lent them a manuscript of this book, which, at that time was incomplete. As they saw what the Bible said about the outpouring of the Holy Spirit, they began to reach out. What happened? They were gloriously filled - just as the Scripture says.

STREAMS OF LIVING WATER

As my friends prayed with me, I began to believe and to thank God for the gift of his Spirit. Then they said to me, "Now just speak in tongues." "Oh no!" I thought. "If I try and do that I'll say "blublublublublub", then dry up and feel like an idiot." At first I was not prepared to step out in faith and risk the embarrassment if nothing happened. But then, as faith started to rise, I broke the sound barrier and spoke in tongues.

Remember, God doesn't speak in tongues, you do! Initially, I did not realize this. I sat there waiting for God to speak through me in some mystic way. But I had to take the first step. I had to operate my diaphragm and vocal chords. I had to speak – with the Spirit's enabling.

The Old Testament tells us the story of a woman who had run out of oil. Elisha told her:

> **Go outside, borrow vessels from all your neighbors,**
> **empty vessels and not too few. Then go in and shut**
> **the door behind youself and your sons and pour into**

**all these vessels. And when one is full, set it aside
(2 Kings 4:3,4).**

This woman could have thought, "That's daft. If I tip this little drop of oil I have left from this jar into that one, I'll just have a little drop in there instead." It could be argued that the miracle did not happen when she started to pour, it happened when she continued pouring and the oil kept flowing and multiplying. How similar to speaking in tongues!

As I prayed on in tongues I began to have serious doubts about what I was doing and a spiritual battle started to rage inside.

"You're just making this all up, Terry," the devil argued. "There's nothing supernatural about this. It's just a lot of rubbish." I wanted God - not something unreal. But as I listened to myself making these funny noises, I was frightened of fooling myself that I had something genuine when it was not. So I stopped speaking. My friends had to encourage me to recognize the enemy and to overcome my doubts, fears and unbelief.

The devil does not want Christians to be filled with the power of the Holy Spirit. It is therefore not surprising that he stirs up so much controversy about the subject, and tries to discourage any who reach out in faith. Tongues does sound weird, but so too do many of the world's languages. Sometimes when I'm abroad I hear the strangest sounds from people's mouths! I ponder: Is that a language?!" They answer my question by communicating with one another in it! So when you speak in tongues, don't try to analyze your vocabulary and recognize the enemy's temptation to doubt. I had a battle but I got through it – and so can you.

**Submit yourselves therefore to God. Resist the devil,
and he will flee from you (James 4:7).**

Phil Rogers' battle over tongues was similar to mine. He wanted to be filled with the Spirit on God's terms, not his, and decided that if tongues was part of the deal, then he would have to have that as well.

As they prayed for him to be baptized in the Spirit, someone told him that the Lord was saying, "Open your mouth and I will fill it." They continued to encourage him to step out in faith and speak in tongues. But he just stood there with his mouth open, waiting for something to happen and thinking, "Perhaps my tongue will start thrashing about inside my mouth of its own accord." Then some wise person said, "In Acts 2 we read that they began to speak in other tongues as the Spirit enabled them. Once you start speaking, the Holy Spirit will give you the words and the flow will come."

He began thinking of the disciples in the boat on the sea (Matt.

14:28,29). He imagined Peter looking at the raging water and then at Jesus standing there inviting him to "Come". The only way he would know if the waves would hold him up was to get out of the boat and try walking on them. Phil stood there for what seemed like an eternity of self-consciousness, and then he started to speak out odd words like those around him. The initial trickle became a great surge and he suddenly found himself caught up in a great flow of tongues.

TONGUES FOR All

Simon the Sorcerer was evidently impressed by something when he saw the Samaritan believers receive the Spirit (Acts 8:18). Clearly, there IS some outward manifestation when people are filled with the Spirit. Speaking in tongues seems to be the most common occurrence, although prophecy is sometimes mentioned (Acts 19:6).

Some people question, "Does everyone speak in tongues?"

Read Acts 2:4, 10:44-46, 19:6,7 and 1 Corinthians 14:23.

Note the frequency of the word "all" in respect of speaking in tongues.

Certainly, not everyone is required to speak in tongues in a public context, but God wants us all to use tongues in a private capacity.

Maybe you have already been baptized in the Holy Spirit but have never spoken in tongues.

The devil "comes to steal and kill and destroy"; Jesus wants to give us "life ... to the full" (John 10:10). These two individuals are opposed to one another. Jesus wants only what is good for you and freely offers you the gift of tongues. Ask him for it. Step out in faith. Speak out and you will discover that the Holy Spirit will give you the enabling.

When I finally left all my doubts and fears behind me and poured out my praise in tongues, I felt a surge of power go right through my body. For the first time in my Christian life I experienced the intimacy of the cry, "Abba Father". Suddenly I knew that he was right there with me and I loved him in a way that I had never loved him before.

Gone was my old reluctance to speak about Jesus to others. Now I wanted to tell them about him. And I wanted to explore the other spiritual gifts available to the believer too. I had been brought into an exciting supernatural dimension and was hungry for more. The baptism of the

Spirit was not so much a goal as a gateway of discovery, which would lead on to many more good things ahead.

Peter said that the promise of the Spirit is for all whom the Lord our God will call (Acts 2:39). If you know that you are a believer, you have a promise to claim. Jesus wants to fill you with the Holy Spirit. If you are thirsty, hear his invitation to you, "Come to me and drink." Come with expectation. Ask him for the Spirit. Receive the Spirit. Take a step of faith and speak out. Streams of living water will flow from within you.

Having received the Holy Spirit, you may have the opportunity to counsel others to receive. If so, see the notes in the Appendix.

SPEAKING IN TONGUES

My early opinion of the gift of tongues is reflected in the prayer I prayed when I was a nineteen-year-old student. "Oh Lord, please fill me with your Spirit, but skip the tongues!" At the time, I was kneeling in my study-bedroom in a hall of residence in Bristol. I had become a Christian at the age of fourteen. Now I was at university and was eager to serve God in my new situation.

Some Christians invited me to a half night of prayer, which I attended with a great sense of anticipation. I had been to many prayer meetings but this was different. Never had I experienced such a sense of God's presence in a meeting before. It was the leader who particularly provoked me. He had not been a Christian very long and belonged to a denomination that I did not view very charitably. But when he prayed, he spoke to God with such intimacy and reality that stirred up great yearnings within me. I found myself longing to know God as he did.

I got to know him and discovered his secret. He had been baptized with the Holy Spirit and spoke in tongues. I had already heard about the baptism of the Holy Spirit and had read a number of books about it. Indeed, my pastor back home in London had quietly admitted to praying in tongues in private. So I accepted that the experience was biblical and that it was for today's pastors. But when I began to encounter people of my own age who were involved in these things, I started feeling terribly thirsty.

Certainly, I was privileged to have been brought up in a Christian family. But in spite of that, and in spite of all the sound teaching and enthusiastic activity, I knew that I lacked something. My God lived in unapproachable transcendent glory! I longed to be close to him, to have his Spirit inside me. But I dared not reach out because I was hung up on speaking in tongues.

This gift offended me. I could not see the point of speaking words that I could not understand. And I was frightened that the Spirit would, like some alien brain invader, take me over and control my life.

I was not the first or the last person to have such anxieties. Maybe you share them today. Let's look more closely at the gift and see what the word of God says about it.

NEW LANGUAGES

"These signs will accompany those who believe," said Jesus to his disciples. "They will speak in new tongues." Tongues, healing, miraculous protection and the authority to drive out demons were seen as evidences that God's power was with his people (Mark 16:17,18). Even after the apostles had died, these signs continued for many years. Then they became less common and finally, for 1600 years, all but disappeared.

We are living at an exciting time, a time of church restoration. God is moving among his people and we are again seeing manifestations of his power both in our own nation and throughout the world. One of these manifestations is "new tongues". An increasing number of Christians are beginning to speak in languages that are totally new and unfamiliar – to them.

TONGUES AT PENTECOST

On the day of Pentecost, the believers who were assembled in the upper room spoke in "other tongues" (Acts 2:4). The crowds who gathered to listen heard their own native languages being spoken by working class Galileans!

What was their reaction? (Acts 2:12,13)

In the other accounts of the outpouring of the Holy Spirit, tongues were not generally understood by the bystanders. On those occasions there was not the international context that we see on the day of Pentecost when the languages were recognized by the hearers.

What were the disciples declaring?

Clearly, the disciples were not preaching to the crowd. As they were speaking in their unlearned languages, the bystanders found themselves eavesdropping on Psalm-like declarations.

TONGUES IN CORINTH

Read 1 Corinthians 14:2-5 and consider the following:

When people speak in tongues, to whom are they speaking?

What sorts of things are they saying?

How do they do this?

How does speaking in tongues benefit them?

What did Paul think about Christians speaking in tongues?

Paul wrote this section of his letter because he wanted to correct the Corinthians' misuse of tongues. Today we do not suffer the misuse of tongues so much as the disuse of tongues! So we must keep in mind the context of his comments. We misinterpret Paul if we think that he is either undervaluing tongues or dismissing the practice.

According to Paul, how important is speaking in tongues? (1 Cor. 14:18)

When Paul refers to his speaking in the "tongues of angels" (1 Cor. 13:1), he is probably speaking rhetorically. In other words, he is saying, "If I speak in tongues – whatever language it might be (even if it were the very language of angels), but do not have love, then all I am is a resounding gong or a clanging cymbal." Even angelic languages without love are futile.

PRAYING WITH MY SPIRIT

Paul says:

if I pray in a tongue, my spirit prays but my mind is unfruitful (1 Cor. 14:14).

When we speak in tongues, our prayer bypasses conscious thought and comes directly from our human spirit. At first, this can seem really strange because we discover that we can pray in tongues while our minds are preoccupied with numerous other things. In the context of a meeting it is possible to pray in tongues and think about the Sunday lunch, plan what to do in the afternoon and arrange the schedule for the week. When we pray in tongues we clearly need to discipline our thoughts and focus on the Lord.

One young man who had received the Spirit and spoken in tongues was terrified that his experience had been of the devil. He found that by leaving it empty the devil was stirring up all sorts of filth. Then, I told him how to focus his mind on Jesus and prayed for him. At the meeting later that day he was worshiping the Lord in tongues with a huge grin on his face.

Read 1 Corinthians 14:15.

What was Paul's practice?

God wants to hear us glorify him in our own language and in his. In our regular devotional times we can switch naturally from one to the other whenever we pray or praise the Lord. In our own language we pray rationally about things we know and understand. In tongues we pray about things that are given to us by God and answered by him.

LORD, HELP US TO PRAY

It may sound peculiar to pray prayers and get answers to prayers when we have no idea of their content. Paul gives us some insight into this.

Read Romans 8:26-27.

In what way does Paul say that we are weak? How does the Spirit help us in our weakness?

The Spirit is always willing to pray - even when our flesh is weak. When Paul says, "He intercedes for us" he means that the Spirit prays, not for us, but through us. When we pray in tongues or groan in prayer we are interceding according to the will of God. We may not understand what we are saying but we can be sure that our prayers are accomplishing God's purposes.

Tongues are a great help when we do not know what or how to pray. When we begin interceding in tongues, we may find that we are very moved. The Spirit may give us strong feelings: groanings, pleadings, anger, burdens, and aggression... on occasions we may even weep. After a time of such dynamic praying, there may be a sense of breakthrough and release – a conviction that we have been heard and that God is going to act.

GIVING PRAISE AND THANKS

Luke tells us that at Pentecost the disciples were praising God in tongues (Acts 2:11). Paul talks about our praising God and giving thanks with our spirits (1 Cor. 14:16). Although no one except the Lord understands what we are saying, we could easily be giving thanks when we pray in tongues (v. 17).

There are times when we simply run out of words that are adequate to express praise to the Lord. Tongues go beyond our mental limitations and offer him an expression of sublime praise from our spirits. From time to time we will have feelings of great glory, exhilaration, wonder, awe, reverence, love and adoration. Our worship may be accompanied by tears of joy.

My initial fear of being taken over and of not being in control has proved groundless. I think it arose from the reference to tongues as "ecstatic utterances" or "languages of ecstasy".

What does Paul say in 1 Corinthians 14:32?

This means that when we speak in tongues or prophesy we are always in control of our actions and emotions. We can stop whenever we wish and we can choose to respond emotionally or not. Much of the time we pray in tongues without any feelings at all – as we do in our own language. In fact most of the time praying and praising in tongues is a very normal, down to earth sort of practice.

People who cry out or behave in an abnormal way cannot blame the Holy Spirit. They choose to react like that and are responsible for their conduct. The Spirit does not give us weird and mystical "ecstatic experiences". But he does live in us and intercede for us according to

God's will. If we pause to think about it, that is quite an amazing idea for us to grasp.

SPEAKING IN TONGUES TODAY

Before the twentieth century, the experience of speaking in tongues had become generally regarded by Christians as peculiar to the New Testament era and of no relevance for us today. Then, in December 1900, a group of students at Bethel Bible College in Topeka, Kansas, were given the task of searching the Scriptures to see what they taught about the Baptism in the Holy Spirit. When the founder of the college, a Methodist evangelist called Charles Parham, returned from a three-day preaching trip, he found the students very excited with their discoveries.

That evening they met together to pray that they would be baptized in the Spirit and speak in tongues – just like the disciples on the day of Pentecost. One of the students pointed out that in the New Testament the Spirit had often been received through the laying on of hands and suggested that they try this. At first Parham refused, *but* after praying a little longer, he decided to take God at his Word and step out in faith. He asked one of the students, Agnes, to sit in the center of the room. As he laid his hands on her head "a glory fell upon her, a halo seemed to surround her head and face" and she began to speak in tongues. Parham and many of his students were similarly filled with the Spirit.

In the face of much hostility, this New Testament teaching was passed on. Today, millions of Christians throughout the world have believed and experienced the baptism of the Spirit and can speak in tongues. They will never regret the day when they reached out in faith and received the promise from God.

ABOUT SPIRITUAL GIFTS

In recent years Christians who have been baptized with the Holy Spirit have generally been known as Charismatics. The term comes from the Greek word *charismata*. *Charis* means "grace", so *charismata* are "grace things" or "free gifts" – gifts that the Lord delights to give us even though we do not deserve them. Paul uses the word in Romans 12 and in 1 Corinthians 12 - the two main New Testament passages about spiritual gifts.

There are varieties of gifts (1 Cor. 12:4).

Having gifts that differ according to the grace given to us (Rom. 12:6).

Charismatic Christians have discovered that the gifts of the Spirit were not intended just for New Testament times, but for today as well.

The word, "charismata" is not used for Spiritual gifts alone; it also refers to salvation itself - the greatest free gift of all (see Rom. 6:23).

Read 2 Timothy 1:6,7.

What sort of spirit (Spirit) did Timothy receive?

Since the "gift of God" was received through the laying on of hands, it could refer to the Holy Spirit himself. Certainly he is a wonderful free gift of God's grace that we do not deserve nor could ever earn. Alternatively it may refer to the special gifting that Timothy received when he was appointed as Paul's companion (see 1 Tim. 4:14). Either way, when we receive the gift of the Spirit, we also receive the gifts that the Spirit brings with him.

Read 1 Peter 4:10.

How should we use "whatever gift we have received "?

Note the two types of gift that Peter mentions.

We shall call these gifts of revelation and gifts of power, for in order to speak words from God we need the Spirit's revelation, and in order to serve the needs of others we need the Spirit's power. We will be looking at each of these in the next two chapters. But before we do that, we will examine Paul's teaching about spiritual gifts in Romans 12.

Read verses 3-8.

What do we not all have?

What do we all have?

On what basis are they given?

How are we to use them?

Paul wrote similar things to the Corinthians about our being part of Christ's body.

Read 1 Cor. 12:12-21.

ONE BODY OF MANY DIFFERENT PARTS

We are all individual parts of the body of Christ, the church, and every member has a different role to play. God gives us all the appropriate gifts and abilities that we need and fits each one of us into our own particular place with our own special function. I love the way Paul describes this in Ephesians 2:10 and in the second half of Philippians 3:12:

For we are his workmanship, created in Christ Jesus

for good works, which God prepared beforehand, that we should walk in them. (Eph. 2:10)

I press on to make it my own, because Christ Jesus has made me his own. (Phil. 3:12b)

God wants us to do the works that he has prepared for us in eternity. When we do what God has given us to do, we act with faith. But when we try to do things for which we are not gifted, we cannot do them in faith because God has not given us the grace we need to accomplish them. Then we find ourselves striving in the flesh and failing to achieve the purposes of God.

Consider the seven gifts that Paul mentions in Romans 12:6-8.

This is just a small sample of the many ways in which we can serve the Lord and each other as members of the body of Christ. Some of these gifts may not seem particularly spiritual. The first certainly needs some special inspiration of the Spirit. But the fifth seems to be more dependent on financial circumstances, the fourth, on personality and the third and sixth on developed abilities.

Don't be too spiritual about these things. People often get confused and uptight about identifying their spiritual gifts and the role that God has for them in the church. God has created us as we are and wants us to be ourselves. Our natural abilities, our gifts and our achievements are just as much God-given as things like speaking in tongues. God calls us to be what he created us to be and to do what we can do best. One of my favorite texts is Ecclesiastes 9:10.

Consider the first part of this verse.

Life is too short to mess around wasting time. If something needs doing and you think you can do it, don't worry whether it is your gifting or not - just get on with it. If you are not meant to be involved in this particular thing, you will not be very successful at it. But that does not matter. Next time you can let someone else have a go.

All too often we talk about our giftings as strengths and our lack of them as weaknesses. This is unhelpful. By attaching emotional terms particularly to our so-called failures we only make ourselves feel inadequate and defensive. So get stuck in and do whatever comes to hand. By trial and error you will soon discover what you can and cannot do in faith.

MANIFESTATIONS OR ENDOWMENTS

The classic passage on spiritual gifts is, of course, 1 Corinthians 12.

Read verses 1 to 11.

In verse 1 Paul introduces us to the subject of "spiritual gifts". He does not use "charismata" but a different word that can be literally translated "spirituals". "Spirituals" are things that have to do with the Spirit - what he does and the way he operates.

Paul did not want the Corinthians to be ignorant about the ways in which the Holy Spirit works in the church. He therefore described how the Spirit gives us various gifts (v. 4) and different ways of serving (v. 5) and how he works in such diverse ways (v. 6). Then in verse 7 Paul made a statement, which is essential to our proper understanding of these things.

To each is given the manifestation of the Spirit for the common good. (1 Cor. 12:7)

Paul listed nine ways in which the Holy Spirit manifests himself. These manifestations are usually referred to as the gifts of the Spirit. The list is representative, not exclusive, since such things as visions and dreams, mentioned in Acts 2: 17, are not included here even though they are clearly the same type of phenomenon.

To be completely accurate we should call these things manifestations of the Spirit, because they are not strictly gifts. If someone gives me a gift for my birthday it is mine. I own it and keep it with my other possessions. It is at my disposal to use whenever and wherever I choose. But we cannot treat the Spirit's manifestations like this.

What exactly is a manifestation? It is a means by which the Holy Spirit manifests or reveals himself. It is something that makes evident his presence and power. In many church services nothing extraordinary happens because nobody expects the Holy Spirit to manifest himself in a powerful way. The congregation assumes that he is among them simply because he is omnipresent. But they do not worry much about it. They just plod on as usual.

This sort of service is totally alien to the New Testament. When the early Christians met together they had a personal awareness that the Spirit was with them and saw clear evidence of his work among them. They would never have imagined it possible to meet without there being any sense of the Spirit's presence or any manifestations of his power! If this had happened, they would have been on their faces seeking the Lord, searching their hearts, repenting of sin and crying out for the Spirit to move afresh among them.

How tragic it is to see many of our present day churches meeting week after week oblivious of these things! Some are even hostile to the very idea that the Spirit should manifest himself in their services.

RECEIVING MANIFESTATIONS

In 1 Corinthians 12 there are three principles, which from the basis upon which the Holy Spirit manifests himself in the church.

SOVEREIGNTY OF THE SPIRIT

Read 1 Corinthians 2:10,11.

What does the Holy Spirit do and know?

Since the Spirit is in touch with God and with the church, he can at his own discretion, give manifestations according to the need of the moment. So what happens when the church meets together?

The Holy Spirit reveals his presence and power among us by distributing to individuals the various manifestations mentioned in the 1 Corinthians 14 list. He makes a sovereign choice to give a prophecy to this person and a vision to that one, a gift of healing to another and word of knowledge to a fourth. We cannot work to order because we do not possess these things as gifts. The Spirit controls their use and decides who has them and when.

BENEFIT OF THE BODY

The Spirit does not give someone a manifestation for his or her own benefit, but for the common good (1 Cor. 12:7).

Read 1 Corinthians 14:12 and consider the gifts in which
we should try to excel.

These believers were keen to see the Holy Spirit working in the
church and Paul encouraged them to pursue the "gifts" that edify (1 Cor.
14:4,5,17) and strengthen (1 Cor. 14:3,26) others.

God wants you to be motivated not by personal ambition, but by a
desire to see the church built up. Is that your aim? Then be available to
the Spirit and move out in faith when he prompts you.

EAGER DESIRE

What, according to 1 Corinthians 12:31 and 14:1a, should
we eagerly desire?

The manifestations of the Spirit will not be given to the satisfied,
the indifferent and the unbelieving. They will come to those who covet
and value them, to those who long to see the church strengthened, the
purposes of God fulfilled and the name of Jesus glorified.

Read Matthew 7:11 and James 4:2,3.

To whom does God give good gifts?

Why don't we receive good gifts from God?

If you put aside your own desires and seek the blessing of the church
as a whole, then God will be happy to manifest himself through you. So if
you have received the baptism of the Spirit, don't sit back as if you have
arrived. You have not. Be diligent. Seek God earnestly. Ask him to give
you his "gifts". Put yourself at his disposal. Be eagerly available at any
time - especially when you join others to worship.

THE MANIFESTATIONS OF THE SPIRIT

Here is a list of the various manifestations of the Spirit that we find mentioned in the New Testament. It has been taken largely from 1 Corinthians 12:8-10.

- Word of wisdom

- Word of knowledge

- Faith

- Visions

- Dreams

- Working miracles

- Healing

- Discerning of spirits

- Interpretation of tongues

- Interpretation of dreams and visions

- Prophecy

- Tongues

- Deliverance

Some of these involve a revelation from the Spirit that is then spoken out, while others involve a supernatural empowering.

Have a look at the list and consider those you think could be called "gifts of revelation". We shall be describing them in the next chapter.

GIFTS OF REVELATION

PROPHECY

This is the most frequently mentioned of the spiritual gifts. Much could be written about it, but here we will limit ourselves to such manifestations of prophecy that any member of the body may receive and which we are all encouraged to eagerly desire. Paul wrote about prophecy in 1 Corinthians 14:1-5 and 26-33.

> Read these passages through again and notice particularly what is said about prophecy.

When someone prophesies, he is essentially acting as a divine spokesman. He is speaking words that are not his own but which are given to him by the Lord. For this reason, we must not treat prophesying casually. On the other hand, we must not be so afraid of misinterpreting the Lord that we avoid it altogether.

> Read 1 Corinthians 13:9 and note what we must remember about prophecy.

No prophecy will ever be 100 percent from the Lord. It will always be limited by our sensitivity to him, our ability to express ourselves, our theological views, and our preconceived ideas. So when we prophesy, we will be genuinely speaking from God, but will be bringing in a lot of ourselves too.

> According to 1 Thessalonians 5:20, what must we not do with prophecy?

> According to 1 Corinthians 14:29, what must we do with it?

God does not want us to think, "Oh, that's just Fred!" neither does he want us to assume that every word is Spirit-inspired. In spite of our limitations, God does speak his word through those of us who are eager to be used in this way.

Read 1 Corinthians 14:1,39.

With reference to prophecy, what does Paul want us to do?

EAGERLY DESIRE IT

Ask God for a prophecy. It may help to ask someone to pray for you to prophesy. I received my first prophecy when I was sitting in a small group. Someone laid hands on me and prayed for the Lord to speak through me. For a few moments I had no thoughts at all but then a simple phrase came clearly into my mind.

SPEAK OUT IN FAITH

I took a step of faith and began to speak out the phrase that had come to mind. As I spoke, more words came and then they flowed and flowed – just like the first time I spoke in tongues. I was amazed as I listened to myself because my words were so relevant to my situation at the time. My first prophecy was a word of encouragement just for me.

SPEAK NORMALLY

It is not more spiritual to speak in old-fashioned English or to punctuate your prophecy with liberal doses of "thus says the Lord". Don't do strange things – huff and puff or shake your head. Don't speak in an odd way and get louder as you continue. These things do not enhance your message, so speak naturally.

BE SENSITIVE

Sometimes we may get physical sensations like a thumping heartbeat, butterflies in the stomach, sweaty hands or trembling in our arms and legs. This could be the Spirit prompting us to speak out in faith, or just plain nerves. As we become more sensitive to the Spirit, these feelings often decrease and may even disappear altogether.

We need to work out whether the prophecy is intended for others or is a personal word to us. We must also consider whether the content is appropriate at that particular time. The fact that we receive it now does not mean we have to say it now. We may have to hold the prophecy and let it settle in our hearts until a more suitable moment arrives.

DON'T ABUSE IT

In 1 Corinthians 14:3 Paul specifies three purposes of prophecy. What are they?

Prophecy is not for rebuking the church, nor is it for off-loading our frustrations or current gripes. If we prophesy without love, we are nothing (1 Cor. 13:2). We must be prepared to have our contribution weighed (1 Cor. 14:29) and be willing to receive correction as is necessary.

VISIONS

Compare Acts 2: 17, 1 8 with Numbers 12:6. With what are visions and dreams associated?

God wants to give his people visions and dreams. A vision is most commonly a picture in the imagination; a fleeting image given by the Spirit. This may on occasions be a vivid picture that we "see" in full Technicolor. People have had visions when their eyes have been open too. They have seen angels, evil spirits and invisible words written on foreheads.

When we receive a vision we can usually understand and explain its meaning, but sometimes we may be completely stumped. Then we must allow someone else to make sense of it for us. This manifestation of the Spirit is very similar to tongues and interpretation.

Read Daniel 5:5, 26-28.

DREAMS

The Bible makes no great distinction between dreams and visions.

According to Job 33:15, what is a dream?

The main difference between a vision and a dream is that you are awake when you have a vision but asleep when you have a dream. When Jacob set out for Egypt he had a vision, not a dream – because he was awake when God spoke to him (Gen. 46:2). We are unlikely to have dreams during meetings because we do not sleep at those times!

Visions tend to edify others while dreams tend to edify you. Dreams may even be life-changing.

What did Joseph do in response to a dream? (Matt. 1:24)

Early in our marriage my wife was troubled with a fear that I might die. One night she had an incredible dream in which she saw the Lord on his throne and Jesus' second coming. It was so vivid that it not only delivered her from her fears but gave her a whole new perspective on eternity as well.

Other examples of dreams in the Bible can be found in Genesis 20:3-7, 1 Kings 3:5-15, Daniel 2, and Matthew 2:19-20.

Dreams, like visions, may need interpretation. Clearly we must be careful not to become preoccupied with the meaning of dreams – as men in the past have done. And we must not be sucked into the modern psychological interpretation of dreams either. The Bible distinguishes between ordinary dreams and specific messages from God.

According to Ecclesiastes 5:3, when do dreams come?

We must beware of looking for hidden meanings in every dream that we remember. If it comes from God, we will be aware that it has been given to us and understand its purpose.

WORDS OF KNOWLEDGE

Sometimes the Holy Spirit gives us information that we did not know and, humanly speaking, could never have known. It is a very useful tool in counseling. The Spirit impresses thoughts on the counselor's mind and enables them to get to the root of a person's problems and bring resolution to them. The knowledge usually comes through words, but it may also come in pictorial or other forms.

While counseling a young woman with chronic asthma I saw a fleeting image of a white statue of an angel in the middle of a lot of nettles. As I described this to her she suddenly burst into tears. The Lord had given me a glimpse of her mother's grave. This exposed the root of her problems and enabled us to minister healing to her.

Words of knowledge may also be given in public meetings. The Spirit reveals information or brings images to mind. He may even give us a physical sensation, such as a feeling of sudden pain in a certain part of our body, indicating that someone present has a problem in that region. The Lord may even show us the person in the congregation to whom such a word of knowledge applies. Naturally, before we speak out, we do need to check that the pain is not ours!

Sometimes we may receive a word that would expose or embarrass someone. Then we must be extremely sensitive and caring. When sharing such things publicly it would be better not to demand an immediate response but to invite whomever it might be to see you privately after the meeting.

Jesus used a word of knowledge when he spoke to the woman of Samaria.

What two things did he tell her? (John 4:18)

What did she tell the Samaritans? (v. 29)

Such revelations tell us that God knows about our situation and that he wants to encourage, help, release or heal us. When such a word is shared publicly and when someone responds, the faith of the whole group is stirred.

WORDS OF WISDOM

Closely related to a word of knowledge is "a word of wisdom". This is not the wisdom that we acquire through experience, but a revelation of the Spirit who tells us what to do or say in a specific, often difficult, situation. This manifestation is often needed in leaders' decision-making meetings, in confrontation situations or in counseling. Jesus used the word of wisdom when the Pharisees tried to trap Him.

Read Matthew 22: 17-22.

What were Jesus' words of wisdom? How did the Pharisees react?

Read Luke 12:12.

When will we need wisdom from the Spirit?

Other possible examples can be found in Acts 6:1-7, 15:28-29 and 27:10,31.

INTERPRETATION OF TONGUES

Some people who work as interpreters are fluent in several languages. Their skills are in great demand. The manifestation of interpretation of tongues is quite different from a learned ability to interpret. When someone speaks aloud in tongues, the Spirit will inspire someone else (and sometimes the original speaker) to translate, interpret or explain it to the people in the meeting.

When God wants you to interpret tongues, you will not understand what the speaker is saying but words will start coming into your mind and you will have the distinct impression that the Spirit is revealing their meaning to you. Since the language will most likely be foreign to everyone, no one will ever be completely sure that your interpretation is accurate. You must take a step of faith, speak out and let others weigh your words.

For one who speaks in a tongue speaks not to men but to God; for no one understands him, but he utters mysteries in the Spirit (1 Cor. 14:2).

What response is desirable from the listener? (v. 16)

An utterance in tongues will generally be a prayer or an exclamation of praise addressed to God rather than a message from God to us. We would therefore generally expect an interpretation of tongues to reflect this Godward movement. Sometimes, however, we hear interpretations given like prophecies (e.g. "My people, I alone am to be your heart's desire. Let your soul long after me as a deer pants after the water brooks").

If the original tongue was spoken to God then the interpreter has turned round his interpretation. Let us turn it back again: "O Lord, You alone are my heart's desire. My soul longs after you as a deer pants after the water brooks." See how this lifts the spirit. Instead of feeling that God is demanding something of us, we find ourselves identifying with the one speaking in tongues, caught up with his praise and able to say "Amen!"

Some interpretations are turned round like this because of preconceived notions that a "message in tongues" requires an interpretation that sounds like a prophecy.

When we are waiting for an interpretation of tongues, the silence can make us all rather tense. Paul encourages us not to be passive at this point.

one who speaks in a tongue should pray for the power to interpret (1 Cor. 14:13).

God wants us to overcome our uncertainties and fears and reach out in faith. As we begin to interpret, we will have the joy of lifting the spirits of those around us and of encouraging them in their own prayer and praise.

DISCERNING OF SPIRITS

This gift of revelation enables us to evaluate, identify or distinguish between spirits and is particularly necessary when dealing with powers of darkness. It exposes the demonic so that we can effectively deal with it and bring deliverance to the victim. The Holy Spirit may impress on us the identity of a demon, or give us a visual image, such as a large dark object on a person's shoulders. He enables us to recognize when a demon is speaking through a demonized person and when that person is speaking himself.

Jesus helped the demonized, so too did Paul. We will doubtless be very eager for this manifestation when we encounter the demonized too. (See Matt. 9:32; 17:18, Mark 1:25; 5:8, Acts 16:18.)

In other situations, the Spirit may also give this ability to show us the spiritual source of a person's words, motives or deeds. In meetings he may identify contributions or events that are demonically inspired (e.g. false prophecy), or ones that are purely fleshly and not from the Holy Spirit.

Read 1 John 4:1 and note:

What John encourages us not to believe.

What he encourages us to do.

Why?

GIFTS OF POWER

SPEAKING IN TONGUES

It is impossible to speak in a foreign language, which we have never learned. So when we pray in tongues, we are using a gift of power. If the Spirit can work this miracle in us again and again, then he can certainly give us other manifestations. Speaking in tongues quickens our faith for other works of the Spirit and is often the first step to receiving prophecy, and other gifts of revelation.

When we have received the gift of tongues we can use it privately whenever we wish. We do not need any special prompting from the Spirit nor do we need any interpretation. But when the Spirit provokes someone to speak out loud in tongues during a meeting, then we naturally need an interpretation so that everyone can understand.

In 1 Corinthians 14 Paul discusses tongues in quite some detail.

For who are tongues a sign? (v. 22)

Since the uncontrolled use of speaking in tongues might make such people think we are mad, Paul puts certain restrictions on the use of tongues when the whole church comes together.

Read 1 Corinthians 14:26-28.

How many people should speak in tongues?

How should they speak?

Who must also be present?

Paul does not discourage speaking in tongues when we come together. In fact, he expects there to be such manifestations. If we handle the gift wisely and follow his practical guidelines, unbelievers among us will understand what we are saying and be amazed. Then, when prophecies come that lay bare the secrets of their hearts, they will acknowledge that God is among us.

GIFTS OF HEALING

Paul did not say that God gives us a gift of healing. He used two plural words, "gifts of healing" (1 Cor. 12:9). Some commentators have suggested that every individual healing is a special gift of the Spirit, and that we are totally dependent upon him on every occasion. The Spirit delights to give gifts of grace to those who are sick. To the lame he gives the gift of being able to walk, to the one with cataracts, the gift of clear sight, to the asthma sufferer, the gift of being able to breathe freely. These are his healing gifts to those who are sick.

The Spirit is the Healer. We are like his postmen. Now and again he gives us a healing gift for someone and we simply deliver it. Since a postman is neither the sender nor the owner of his letters and parcels, so no person is the healer or can be said to possess the gift of healing. We are always totally dependent on the Lord – as Jesus was. Luke writes:

the power of the Lord was with him to heal (Luke 5:17).

Healing comes in God's time. Peter and John would often have seen the crippled beggar who sat at the temple gate. But one day, when he asked them for money, the Spirit of God gave them a gift of healing for him instead. They acted upon the prompting of the moment and the man was instantly healed.

> Consider what the following statement should say and check your answer in Acts 3:16.
>
> It is our gift and the faith that comes through us that has given this complete healing to him.

DO ALL HAVE GIFTS OF HEALINGS?

No, we do not. God clearly calls some people to specialize in gifts of healing. A number will have some success, while others will seem not to be particularly gifted in this area. The Christians who do not see much result from their praying for the sick must not, however, assume that the

Spirit will use only those who frequently see the sick healed. The Spirit will often use someone who IS keen, available and willing to step out in faith.

Read Matthew 10:1.

To whom was Jesus speaking? What authority did they have?

Read Luke 10:1,9.

To whom was Jesus speaking? What did he command them to do?

Read Mark 16: 17,18.

To whom is Jesus speaking? With reference to healing, what are they encouraged to do?

HOW TO BE INVOLVED IN HEALING

Someone has calculated that about one fifth of all the verses in the four Gospels relate to healing, deliverance or raising the dead. The phrase, "gifts of healings" implies that there are many different kinds of healing. Jesus did not come to save us from spiritual disability alone. He wanted to see us physically and mentally whole, to give us life to the full. But how do we do his works?

In the Gospels we find Jesus using many different methods to heal. Sometimes he touched or laid hands on the sick. Sometimes he spoke to the sickness. Sometimes he took someone by the hand and raised him up. Sometimes he told people to go and show themselves to the priest. Sometimes he did some very odd things like making a mud pack for a blind man's eyes and sticking his fingers in the ears of a deaf man. We have to conclude that there is no hard and fast, "You do it this way" rule. We are utterly dependent on the Holy Spirit.

When the Spirit gives us a gift of healing for someone we must try to discern how he wants us to pray. Should we lay hands on the sufferer? Should we pray in tongues? Should we address God or rebuke the sickness? Does the Spirit want us to anoint with oil?

Clearly, we must be alert to the Spirit's prompting and then take a step of faith. If we are unwilling to reach out, we are not likely to see anyone healed.

One night my wife had a severe stomachache and could not get to sleep. While she was crying out with the pain I was wondering what on earth I could do. Then, suddenly I began to feel very angry. I rebuked the pain and prayed over her strongly in tongues. She was instantly quiet and soon fell asleep in my arms.

God wants us to reach out to people who are suffering. We do not possess the power the heal them, but he does. All he needs is our availability and willingness to be used. The simplest question, "May I pray for you?" is often all we need to ask. Even unbelievers respond positively to it. They need to see that we, like Jesus, are not concerned simply for their salvation but for their wholeness. God will act - but we must step out in faith and trust him.

Read Hebrews 11:6.

What is it impossible to do?

WORKING MIRACLES

Miracles and healings are very closely allied. In the Gospels the supernatural actions of Jesus, including all kinds of healings, are called miracles (see Mark 6:5). Jesus' miracles also included turning water into wine, calming a storm, walking on water and multiplying food to feed the crowds. Some miracles, like the amazing catch of fish and the finding of a coin in a fish's mouth, are like divinely managed coincidences. Sometimes a miracle will defy natural laws. At other times God's involvement will be clear from what happens in a particular situation.

Paul is probably referring to these types of activities (excluding healing) when he speaks of "miraculous powers" Literally, "workings of powers") in 1 Corinthians 12:10. We also read of miracles in Romans 15:19, Galatians 3:5 and in Hebrews 2:4. We read that:

God has appointed ... miracles (1 Cor. 12:28).

Read Hebrews 2:3,4 and note the purpose of signs, wonders and miracles.

Phil recounts a helpful story, "When we were first married, Sandy and I were given an old twin-tub washing machine. One day while Sandy was using the spin dryer it began to make a strange noise and emit acrid smoke. We unplugged it but there was no use in my trying to mend it because I am not mechanically minded. Then Sandy suggested that I pray for it. I walked out of the room struggling with the absurd idea – which was more of a challenge from the Lord than a request from my wife. I sheepishly returned, laid my hands on the poor old machine and prayed for it. Then I took a step of faith, plugged it in and switched it on. It worked perfectly - no smoke, no smell, no funny noise. We never had any trouble with it again, and it was still working well when we eventually bought a new automatic machine.

FAITH

Hearing with faith - that is the crucial factor in receiving salvation, the Spirit and his gifts (Gal. 3:2,5. Rom. 10:14,17).

Consider the definition of faith in Hebrews 11:1.

We read that God gives "to another faith by the same Spirit" (1 Cor. 12:9). All faith comes by the Spirit, but here Paul is referring to a special manifestation of faith, which is given for a specific occasion. It is a sudden surge of confidence and certainty and often comes in some crisis situation. We suddenly know that what we do not see will come to pass.

What does this faith do? (Matt. 17:20)

Think of three biblical examples of faith (e.g. Elijah calling down fire from heaven).

DELIVERANCE

One in four of all the people that Jesus healed were afflicted by evil spirits.

When Jesus sent his disciples out what did he give them? (Luke 9:1)

Why were they so excited when they returned? (Luke 10: 17)

What is the first sign that will accompany those who believe? (Mark 16:17)

Sometimes a demon may suddenly manifest itself. This happened when Jesus was in the synagogue (Mark 1:23-25). Sometimes the Holy Spirit will enable us to discern the spirits and we will then know that we have the authority to tell them to go.

Read Acts 16:18.

What did Paul say to release the slave girl from the spirit of divination?

By faith, we must do the same. The demons must submit to Jesus. Like Paul, we have the authority and power of the Spirit to speak firmly to them and command them to go.

Read Luke 11:24-26.

How can a person who has been delivered and saved guard against further intrusion from Satan?

When we deal with this subject we must avoid extremes. Some err because they see demons under every chair. They try to cast out spirits when the real problem is to do with the flesh. On the other hand, some categorically declare that Christians cannot possibly be troubled by demons. They leave believers struggling with demonic problems that could have been dealt with by a word of authority.

GIFTS OF POWER IN THE TWENTIETH CENTURY

In today's rational and scientific climate, modern man cannot entertain the idea that demons actually exist, let alone that they affect others. Society suggests that someone is not demonized; he is simply mentally ill or suffering from a perplexing affliction like epilepsy.

The Bible gives another option. It clearly presents to us the realities of a positive and a negative spirit realm. We see the Father, Son, Holy Spirit and angels. But we also see Satan, demons, principalities and powers of darkness. The Christian knows that these spiritual beings are real and that they interact with people on earth,

People in the New Testament expected to see the miraculous. We often encounter it in the so-called Third World. Healings, deliverance and miracles seem to be taking place with great frequency and there are even reports that people are being raised from the dead. Sadly, we in the West seem largely skeptical of these things and our expectation level is low.

Why couldn't Jesus do many miracles in his hometown? (Matt. 13:58)

The problem for the believer tends not to center round a sense of personal weakness: "I find it so hard to believe. I just don't seem to be able to find the faith." It is actually more to do with a positive refusal to accept the truth: "Miracles died out with the apostles. I can't believe that they happen today. I don't believe you and I'm not going to change my mind."

Jesus was grieved at the hardness of men's hearts and could do no mighty miracles when he was in the company of people who had no faith in him. He must react the same way today. Even those of us who believe that the Spirit still gives supernatural manifestations are often infected with disbelief and cynicism.

> According to Mark 16: 14, how did Jesus handle the stubborn unbelief of his disciples when they refused to believe those who had seen him after he had risen from the dead?

Clearly, Jesus wanted the disciples to repent of their unbelief. He longs to see us repent of our unbelief too. Don't allow our worldly-wise, scientific society to dictate to you what you must believe. You serve a God for whom nothing is impossible. Rise up from unbelief and into faith. Be available. Be willing. Move forward.

GIFTS TO THE CHURCH

God gives some giftings on a more permanent basis. We have already looked at the list of gifts in Romans 12. There is another list in 1 Corinthians 12.

> Read verses 27-31 and consider the nine giftings mentioned there.

> What important statement does he make about you? (v. 27)

> Read Ephesians 4:7-13.

In recent years the Holy Spirit has drawn a great deal of attention to this key passage and its relevance for the restoration of the church.

After Jesus had ascended he sat down at his Father's right hand, poured out his Spirit and gave gifts to men.

> Note the gifts that are listed here.

As people have been baptized in the Holy Spirit and have been gifted in various ways, some have discovered that they have been given a specific role in the church.

FIRST APOSTLES, SECOND PROPHETS

Traditionally it has been taught that apostles and prophets existed only in New Testament days. The Bible does not accommodate such a belief. If we say that we need pastors, evangelists and teachers, for what reason do we omit apostles and prophets? The Corinthian and Ephesian passages tell us that apostles and prophets are vitally important for the church in every age.

The comment, "First of all apostles" does not refer to time. It does not mean "in the days of the early church but not later on". Rather, it indicates the priority or importance of these particular ministries. If they were so important to the New Testament church, we dare not try to operate without them today.

> Read Ephesians 2:20 and note what the church is built on.

Some commentators say that this refers to the founding of the early church and conclude that after the original apostles died, their ministry became obsolete. These commentators also seek to back up their argument from Revelation 21:14.

> What is written on the twelve foundations of the wall of the city of God?

The church was initially founded and governed by the twelve apostles, including Matthias who replaced Judas (Acts 1:26, 2:14, 6:2). But very soon other apostles were raised up.

> Note those mentioned in the following verses: Acts 14:14; Rom. 16:7; Gal. 1:19.

Also included among the apostles, although not mentioned as such, were probably Mark, Timothy and Titus. Evidently there were not just twelve apostles but also many more. By the grace of God, they established churches in town after town throughout the Roman Empire and beyond.

What applies to the worldwide church also applies to the local church. In Ephesians 2:20-22, Paul is saying that the apostles lay the foundations on which the whole (global) church is being built. Then he turns his attention to the Ephesian church and includes them in God's plan. During the three years that he had spent with them he had laid the foundation of the local church in Ephesus.

Earlier, he had done exactly the same thing in Corinth.

How did he lay a foundation as an expert builder?
(1 Cor. 3:10)

Paul knew that he had been gifted by God as an apostle. He had the expertise to lay proper doctrinal and structural foundations and had authority to appoint elders. Wherever he went he established churches – with the help of gifted companions like Silas, a prophet, and Timothy (Acts 15:32, 18:5).

In the New Testament each living church was individually built on an apostolic and prophetic foundation. Indeed, a living church cannot be properly established without it. Today it is just as essential for each local church to be built on the foundation of apostles and prophets. That is why the ascended Christ is restoring the baptism and gifts of the Spirit and the gifts of apostles and prophets to his Church.

Apostles and prophets have not been entirely absent in previous generations. Men such as John Wesley and Charles Haddon Spurgeon were undoubtedly gifted apostles even if, in their day, they were not acknowledged as such. Jesus wants to restore all the New Testament giftings, that through them he might build his church in this generation according to the Father's specifications. The goal of these Ephesians 4 ministries is this:

to equip the saints for the work of ministry, for building up the body of Christ, until we all attain to the unity of the faith ... to mature manhood, to the measure of the stature of the fullness of Christ (Eph. 4:12,13).

The fragmented church will become the radiant bride of Christ (Eph. 5:27) only as we recognize the ministries of apostles and prophets and allow them to function in the way that God originally intended.

EQUIPPING THE SAINTS

In the Authorized Version Ephesians 4:12 reads, "for the perfecting of the saints, for the work of the ministry, for the edifying of the body of Christ". This gives the impression that all the work falls on the shoulders of the full-time minister. He has to perfect his flock, do all the work of ministry and edify the body of Christ as well! But this is not at all what Paul meant. The task of leaders is not to put on services for the saints (believers), but rather to equip the saints for service. As Christians then give themselves to the work of serving the body the whole body is strengthened and built up.

If the church is to be fully equipped we must not only have pastors, teachers and evangelists, but apostles and prophets as well. All these ministries also need each other because they work as a team, each complementing and harmonizing with the others.

While apostles and prophets may head the team in their gifting, the others must be brought in if we are to see the local church grow in unity and maturity.

> Note who went to Samaria (Acts 8:14), Antioch (Acts 11:25,26), Phrygia and Galatia (Acts 16:6).
>
> Who were the leaders in the church in Antioch? (Acts 13:1)

In the early church there was always a plurality of elders (see Acts 14:23, 20:17, 1 Tim. 5:17, Titus 1:5, James 5:14 and 1 Pet. 5:1). Today we have drifted away from the biblical norm and instead load one man with the responsibility of leading the church. While the elders share their giftings, the full-time leader struggles alone with limited abilities and is expected to do everything.

If a full-time minister is an evangelist, he will equip his people for outreach. They may see many new converts but will not know how to encourage them and build them up. The pastor is not gifted in this area. But if a church is led by an apostle, a prophet, an evangelist and various pastors and teachers, then they will interact together and the whole church will be edified.

A small local church will not have all these ministries. But it would benefit greatly from at least two full-time leaders, along with regular input from those who have the gifts that it lacks. As the saints are equipped and give themselves to the work of ministry the church will grow. God will then raise up more apostles and prophets, evangelists, pastors and teachers until the whole church reaches unity in the faith and attains the whole measure of the fullness of Christ.

LAYING A FOUNDATION

Read Romans 15:20.

Why did Paul only want to preach the gospel where Christ was not already known?

In those days Paul never needed to re-lay the foundation of a local church. But today God, the architect, is inspecting the church's foundations and he wants them re-established according to his original plan. If our church is not built on apostolic and prophetic foundations, it must be built on something else. What? What does God see as he inspects the foundations? He sees churches that are built on:

INSTITUTIONALISM

In the UK we have an institutional state church. If one of its ministers wants to bring in biblical practices and make changes, he has to make a formal application to do so. He may say "The Bible says... so I'd like to..." but he will probably be told, "That's not the point. You can't do that. We don't allow it in this institution." Although great progress has been made by some local state churches, they always have to battle with problems related to institutional factors.

TRADITION

Take another church where the pastor also wants to make certain changes in order to be more biblical. "It's in the Bible," he says. "So what?" comes the reply. "We've never done it that way before." "But," he protests, "the Bible is our final authority in all matters of doctrine and practice." "Yes," they say, "But we don't do it that way here. We never have done it like that and we don't mean to change. We like things the way they are." Tradition prevails.

SENTIMENT

Another church has for years had a certain organization, which is now ailing and is no longer relevant today. But the leaders cannot bring themselves to close it down. "Old Sid's been doing that for thirty-five years. He'll be ever so upset if we stop it. And his wife plays the piano. We don't want to distress her or we'll have to find another pianist."

DEMOCRACY

In another church the leaders want to give opportunity for personal ministry at the end of each service. But first the idea has to go before the church for a vote. Some of the members, who oppose the present day move of the Spirit, stand against the motion. Then some of the more unspiritual people begin abusing the leadership and stirring up those who feel threatened and apprehensive. The proposal fails to get the necessary majority and thus the church becomes more deeply divided than it has ever been before.

> Read Luke 11:47-49 and note what happens to prophets and apostles.

> Read Jeremiah 1:10 and note why prophets are so unpopular.

When many Christians attend conferences they say, "This is superb teaching. It's such an exciting vision. But we can't do it in our church." Often they cannot do it because their church is built on a wrong foundation. Such churches today are in urgent need of a prophet to reveal what is not of God. When he comes, the people can choose to stone him or hear what he is saying and respond.

BUILDING ON THE FOUNDATION

Churches that have a prophetic vision welcome the prophet and are ready to listen, repent and make necessary changes – just as God's people did in Haggai's day (Haggai 1). The prophet keeps the church sharp and on its toes. The evangelist helps it to take the gospel into the locality. The pastor maintains a caring community and the teacher stimulates a healthy appetite for the truth of God's Word.

We do not all respond to these ministries equally. Some will be keen to follow the evangelist and will be involved in all sorts of evangelistic activities. Some will prefer to care for those who have difficulties. Some will love teaching new converts or bringing prophecies in different situations. Our interest in these things does not make us evangelists, pastors, teachers or prophets, but it does show us where our measure of gifting is likely to he.

We still have not looked at all God's gifts to his church. In Romans 12:7-8 and 1 Corinthians 12:28, Paul mentions others whom God has given special gifts to serve the church.

ADMINISTRATION AND LEADERSHIP

These two terms are quite similar. The first of them is derived from sailing ships. A steersman, captain, or pilot has the ability to give direction, to take charge, to set course and to take the lead. The second literally means "standing in front" and means giving direction, leading, managing, caring for and helping.

How should leaders govern? (Rom. 12:8)

Since elders have oversight of the church, they will obviously require this gift. But others will need it too - when they take charge of meetings, lead worship, direct a group of people or supervise an activity. These leadership, management and administrative skills are vital for a church to run smoothly. The gift involves the ability to organize and motivate people lovingly.

Read John 1 3:12-17, 1 Timothy 4:12 and 1 Peter 5:3 and note how this leadership gift should be exercised.

ENCOURAGEMENT

Encouragement involves coming alongside others to help and fortify them.

Read Acts 9:27, 11:22-25 and 15:35.

How did Barnabas encourage others?

GIVING

Some are given special faith and grace to contribute to the needs of others. The capacity to give financial and material help may come because God gives success in business or a skill in making money. Or it may happen as a result of God's promise to bless those who give so that they can give more (Luke 6:38).

How should givers give? (Rom. 12:8)

HELPING AND SERVING

Helping is a term used to describe what happens when an individual sees someone struggling with something goes over and "takes hold of the other end". Helpers share burdens and are always there to give their support when you need them.

Servants, similarly, are always there when a job needs doing. The servant or steward of a household originally saw to all the practical affairs of running the home. While we must all have a servant heart, some are particularly gifted in serving and getting things done.

According to some commentators, the distinction between these two gifts is that the ministry of helpers is more people oriented while that of servants is more task oriented.

SHOWING MERCY

Paul wrote that the person showing mercy, kindness or compassion should do it with cheerfulness (a Greek word from which we get "hilarity"). People who often give themselves to caring for the sick, the troubled, the bereaved, the weak and the needy can find their spirits becoming affected by the sadness of others and the enormity of the needs. This will make them ineffective. Along with their practical support, they need to bring a cheery disposition that will bring a ray of light, comfort and hope to the suffering.

OTHER GIFTS

Sometimes it is difficult to determine whether we are exercising a general responsibility or a specific gifting. It probably depends on the extent to which we are involved. Sometimes such things as hospitality and intercession are described as gifts.

Read Romans 12:13 and 1 Peter 4:9 and note what we are all exhorted to do.

Paul said that we should also:

> **praying at all times in the Spirit, with all prayer and supplication. To that end keep alert with all perseverance, making supplication for all the saints (Eph. 6:18).**

According to 1 Timothy 2:1, what should be made for everyone?

Clearly, we must not excuse ourselves from these things by saying, "That's not my gift." We are all meant to be involved in them. Undoubtedly, some in the church will be noted for their hospitality and others for their prayer life. While these are not specified as gifts in the New Testament, some people do seem able to exercise them with a degree of faith that surpasses most of us. So maybe we can consider them as gifts.

Creative abilities such as music, drama, dance, graphic arts needlework, painting and writing, are often considered to be spiritual gifts. Craftsmanship and musical skills are mentioned in the Old Testament (Exod. 35:30-35, 1 Chron. 15:16-22). Dorcas used her needlework ability to help the poor (Acts 9:36,39). Let us devote to God whatever skills or gifts we have received from him. Let us be grateful for them, pray for his help as we use them, and serve one another with faith and by the power of the Spirit.

GO ON BEING FILLED

They're drunk!" That is what some of the people in the crowd said when they heard the disciples praising God in tongues on the day of Pentecost. The disciples evidently displayed a happiness and lack of inhibition that suggested that they were intoxicated. Had they been drinking wine - that which makes life merry and gladdens the heart of man (Eccl. 10:19, Ps.104:15)? Was it oil that made their faces shine like that? No, it was the new wine of the Spirit, the fresh anointing oil running down from the head of the church – Christ.

The effects of alcohol soon wear off often leaving a heavy feeling that makes people want more to drink. Excess leads to drunkenness, confusion and loss of control.

What does Paul say that drunkenness leads to? (Eph. 5:18)

What does this word mean? (You may need to look it up.)

The newness of life that we have in Christ is too precious to waste on happiness that will not last. God wants us to be filled with the Spirit.

In Ephesians 5:18 Paul uses a continuous tense that could be translated "be being filled" or "go on being filled" with the Spirit.

When we receive the baptism of the Spirit we do not sit back and think that we have arrived, that we are now living in all the fullness of God. We need to have fresh fillings of the life, love, power and joy of the Spirit.

A few weeks after the disciples" experience at Pentecost, Peter and John were brought before the Sanhedrin and told not to speak in the name of Jesus. When they were released, they joined the other believers for a prayer meeting (Acts 4:23-31).

What did they ask God to give them? How did they want Jesus to demonstrate his power?

The disciples were faced with new challenges and needed a fresh empowering from the Spirit. They did not pray that God would baptize them with his Spirit. He had already done that.

They needed boldness, but they received it by being filled with the Spirit.

Like the disciples, we too face new challenges and need God's power to cope with them. Since boldness, faith, love, joy and peace have their source in the Spirit, it is not surprising that God's answer to our cry, "Please give me more courage ..." may come in the form of a fresh filling with his Spirit.

A FRESH ANOINTING?

The experience of Pentecost was not repeated in Acts 4:31. Many of the disciples present at this later prayer meeting had received the Spirit on the day of Pentecost. Others had doubtless already received the Spirit before this later event. There is only one baptism in the Spirit. The apostle John wrote:

> **the anointing that you received from him abides in you (1 John 2:27).**

The baptism of the Spirit is a once for all experience that can never be repeated. John the Baptist's testimony about Jesus was this:

> **He on whom you see the Spirit descend and remain, is he who baptizes with the Holy Spirit (John 1:33).**

Read 1 Corinthians 6:19.

What is your body?

Where is the Holy Spirit?

From whom did you receive him?

It has become popular to pray for "a fresh anointing" but from the examples above we see that the anointing never left Jesus and never leaves us. We so often want to feel that he is there rather than believe by faith that he is committed never to abandon us.

So when Satan whispers in your ear, "You need a fresh anointing before you can do that," don't listen to him. Remind yourself that you already have the anointing and pray for the help you need to do the task that God has set before you. He may choose to give you a fresh filling of the Holy Spirit, as he did with Peter and the other apostles.

DON'T GRIEVE HIM

The Spirit is a person, so he can be grieved (Eph. 4:30). He is also holy. Unbelievers belong to Satan and display his un-holiness by the way they live. Believers belong to God and must display the Spirit's holiness by they way they live. When we behave in a manner which is inconsistent with our new nature, Satan rejoices but the Spirit is grieved. If we are living in harmony with the Spirit, the slightest sin we commit will rob us of our joy and we will feel the Spirit's sadness.

Jesus came to baptize us with the Spirit and with fire. The Spirit is jealous over us. He blazes against anything that hinders his work in our lives. When we sin through unbelief, disobedience, hardness of heart and the like, we grieve him and quench his fire within us. He remains, but we can lose his dynamic energy.

> Read 1 Thessalonians 5:19 and note what we are exhorted not to do.

> Read 1 Corinthians 6:20 and note what we are exhorted to do.

God wants us to keep short accounts, to confess our sins and repent of them.

> Read Psalm 32:3,4 and note how a guilty person feels.

> Read Psalm 32:1,2 note how a forgiven person feels.

Are you quenching the Spirit in any area of your life? Take this opportunity to question the Spirit about this. Don't harden your heart against him. Respond to his voice. Know the joy of full restoration with the Lord.

STIR UP THE GIFT

"Fan into flame the gift of God, which is in you," said Paul to Timothy (2 Tim. 1:6). How do we do this? By faith. We confess the truth, pray, speak in tongues, worship and reach out believing that God will use us to bless others.

PRAYER

When we get alone with God we take a step of faith. The Bible tells us that we cannot pray as we ought to, but that the Spirit within will help us. As we pray in the Spirit, both in tongues and in our own language, the fire within us is fanned into flame. The more we pray, the hotter it becomes. On sleepy mornings, it is good to remember that Jesus told his weary disciples that the Spirit is always willing to pray, even when the flesh is weak!

WORSHIP

One of my favorite verses is Philippians 3:3. In it Paul describes some of the characteristics of an authentic Christian.

What is the first of these?

He is referring to worship in its broadest sense. Since the Spirit brings joy, peace, thanksgiving and praise, we will stir up the Spirit within us when we take a step of faith and engage in these things. So much the better if we "live joyful" too. The Spirit loves to see not just two-hour praise times, but lives that are characterized by enthusiasm and joy.

Read Ephesians 5:20.

How often we should give thanks to God? For what should we thank Him?

SERVICE

It is said that the devil finds work for idle hands to do. God wants us to occupy ourselves with his work.

Read Romans 12:11.

What must we never lack or keep or do?

Other translations speak of our being "fervent in spirit" (NASB) and "aglow with the Spirit" (RSV). Paul uses the image of water bubbling over a fire. The same phrase is used of Apollos who "spoke with great fervor" or, as the notes in my Bible's margin says, "with fervor in the Spirit" (Acts 18:25).

By faith, let us give ourselves to love and good deeds. Let us care for one another, testify about Jesus, speak his word and use the gifts he has given us. By doing these things, we will continue to keep the Spirit's fire burning and our lives bubbling with zeal for the establishment of God's kingdom on earth.

THE WORK OF THE SPIRIT

The greatest work of the Spirit lies not in the giving of gifts but in the transforming of lives that are having increasing revelation of Jesus, bringing individuals from spiritual darkness into Christ's marvelous light.

There is another very specific work of the Spirit that we need to consider briefly.

Read Romans 15:16; 2 Thessalonians 2:13 and 1 Peter 1:2.

In one word, what is this work?

The Spirit is Holy and part of his divine brief is to make us holy too (1 Thess. 4:3).

According to Romans 8:29, what does God want us to be?

This process continues throughout our earthly lives. As we go through life and experience various trials, faith-testing situations and challenges, the Spirit puts his finger on certain specific areas of ungodly and unrighteous behavior. Then he brings us to repentance, cleansing and change. It is vitally important for us to understand the sanctifying work of the Spirit. He is not out to get us. He is trying to make us like Jesus. It is in our best interests to yield to him and change accordingly.

NO CONDEMNATION

The Bible says that there is

no condemnation for those who are in Christ Jesus (Rom. 8:1).

The devil condemns, the Spirit convicts. The condemnation of the devil goes on day and night. It tends to be vague and makes you feel miserable and hopeless. By sharp contrast, the conviction of the Spirit is always clear and specific. It hurts but makes you feel hopeful. We must learn to reject the one but recognize and respond to the other.

FORGIVE US OUR TRESPASSES

In the Lord's Prayer this plea for forgiveness does not come near the beginning of the prayer, but at the end. This is because it concerns not justification (getting right with God - becoming a Christian) but sanctification (allowing the Spirit to deal with sins in our lives). When we become Christians we are justified by faith in Christ. He makes us 100 percent righteous forever and gives us unrestricted access to the Father

YOU FACE TRIALS

James warns us that we will experience trials. These are sometimes so severe that we may be tempted to think that God has deserted or is punishing us. Job was never given an answer to his suffering and the subject is often shrouded in mystery.

Read Hebrews 12:1-13.

What are the two things that we must not do?

Whom does the Lord discipline and punish?

Why does God discipline?

How does the discipline feel?

What does it produce?

Consider the way you react to trials.

A MAN REAPS WHAT HE SOWS

Church history is littered with people who have been mightily used by God while they have been living in immorality and avarice. We would expect God to withdraw his blessing from these individuals. But he is merciful. He does not use us because we are worthy. He works by grace and will continue to use us even when we sin.

We might be tempted to think that if God is going to use us whether we sin or not, it is almost worth carrying on in sin! We deceive ourselves if we think this. Paul makes it quite plain that whatever we sow we will reap (Gal. 6:7). We may be able to carry on an effective and powerful ministry, but if we are sinning behind the scenes, we will one day reap the consequences.

There's a difference between gifting and holiness. On the one hand, some people do not step out in faith and use their gifts because they think, "I'm not holy enough." On the other hand, some minister powerfully to others while thinking, "It doesn't matter that my life isn't right. God is blessing me anyway." The Lord may not withdraw his power but he will call them to account.

While power operates quite apart from holiness, holiness produces character and a godliness that affects the way in which we minister and use our gifts. We can use God's gifts with the wrong motivation: a desire for recognition or praise, a need for identity or purpose, self-importance, self-promotion, pride or the need to dominate or control others. If our motivation is selfish, our service will have a "clanging cymbal" feel about it. The Corinthians had the gifts, but they needed the love to go with them. So do we.

THE SPIRIT AND THE FLESH

The major area in which we need the constant sanctifying work of the Spirit is in overcoming the flesh.

Paul rebukes the Galatians, "Are you so foolish? Having begun by the Spirit, are you now being perfected by the flesh?" (Gal. 3:3 NASB). Some versions of the Bible unhelpfully translate "by the flesh" as "by human effort" or "by the sinful nature". In Romans Paul makes it plain that when we believe in Christ our old sinful nature dies and we are given a new nature, a new heart that loves righteousness. Our struggle against sin is nothing to do with our trying to overcome our sinful nature that died (Rom. 6:6-7). The battle involves resisting temptation in an earnest desire to live out the righteousness that Jesus has already given to us.

(For a more detailed study of this subject see Terry Virgo's book *God's Lavish Grace*.)

We live in a sinful worldly environment, which tempts us to give in to fleshly desires. The Spirit helps us to overcome these temptations.

> According to Galatians 5:16, what will we not do if we live by the Spirit?

> According to Romans 8:13, what does God want us to do by the Spirit?

Be encouraged! The Spirit will give you the power you need to overcome all temptation.

All over the world Christians are acknowledging their spiritual poverty and are reaching out to Jesus for his power – the baptism of the Holy Spirit. They are receiving his gifts and using them, and God is honoring their faith. The Spirit is equipping them to face difficulties and temptations, working on their lives to conform them to the image of Jesus, building them into a company of men and women who have the power of God and who can wield it against the forces of darkness.

Don't be left out. Don't be an observer when God is blessing and using others so powerfully. God wants you to be involved. "The promise of the Spirit is for you," he says. "And the time to receive is now."

APPENDIX

HELPING OTHERS TO RECEIVE BAPTISM IN THE SPIRIT

Let us suppose that someone comes to you saying. "I want to receive the baptism in the Holy Spirit." Can you lead them into the experience?

Here are a few guidelines:

- Acts 2:38,39 is a key passage. The Holy Spirit is the promise of the Father to everyone who is called. Are they called? Then the promise is for them. Do they understand this? Answer these questions. Don't pray if there is unbelief.

- Allow them to talk and ask questions until they are clear on the subject and say that they confidently expect to receive because of the clear teaching of Scripture and the clear promises of God to them.

- Do not focus too much on tongues. You are not encouraging them to do strange things with their voice, or seek odd feelings.

- You should be exhorting them to reach out in faith to God.

- Pray and encourage them to pray out loud. Listen to their prayer. Are they asking for the Spirit now? Make sure that they are and they are not simply praying around the subject.

- There is sometimes a pause at this point. Ask more questions.

- What is happening? Be cautious - don't give tongues too much or too little importance. Differentiate between the baptism in the Holy Spirit and speaking in tongues. If they believe they have received then don't allow them to get uptight about speaking in tongues. They may receive this gift later.

- However, people who speak in tongues tend to have a greater sense of assurance. Don't tell them that they have received the Spirit, ask them. We cannot impose faith on them. They must be able to reply with faith even if they have not spoken in tongues.

- If they begin to speak in tongues, encourage them not to be satisfied with a quiet mumble. Encourage them to open up their heart to God, to speak out, sing or even shout. They will then have much more opportunity to be aware of having received this dynamic experience.

- The reason for this is that we are not advocating a nice little prayer language, but looking for a praise, which bursts out. Some people are satisfied with too little. They are not receiving a thing but God himself. So encourage them to open up, reach out for more from God and give themselves to God in a new way. Don't let them be too easily content. Encourage them to believe for spiritual gifts.

- If they seem to be having difficulty, don't pressurize them. If there is time, go over any points of which they seem unsure. It is best to make sure that they have understood the truth and that their faith is rising. If you sense that they have not actually come to a place of confident expectation, you may have to postpone praying with them.

- When they have been baptized in the Holy Spirit, follow through. Encourage them by reminding them of what has happened. Help them to be more involved and more expressive in worship - to pray and sing in tongues. Remember that this is all new to them and they need to gain in confidence.

- Look for the development of spiritual gifts and be encouraging. Correct them if necessary. Look for changes in their life and relationship with God. Receiving the baptism in the Holy Spirit should have a powerful and lasting effect.